The
University
as
Publisher

T0324009

◆◆◆◆◆◆◆◆◆◆◆◆◆◆◆◆◆◆◆◆◆◆◆◆◆◆◆◆◆◆◆◆◆◆

The
University
as
Publisher

◆◆◆◆◆◆◆◆◆◆◆◆◆◆◆◆◆◆◆◆◆◆◆◆◆◆◆◆◆◆◆◆◆◆

Edited by Eleanor Harman

UNIVERSITY OF TORONTO PRESS

University of Toronto Press

Diamond Anniversary 1961

Preface

It is doubtless inevitable that a publishing house should celebrate an important anniversary by publishing a book. It is perhaps equally inevitable that such a book should include a description of the founding and growth of the house concerned. However, it is hoped that *The University as Publisher* will serve a much more useful purpose than merely to mark the Diamond Anniversary of the University of Toronto Press.

Although it is the first Canadian university press to have been established, Toronto now has two sister presses, and will, we trust, soon greet several more. This volume may, therefore, be of interest to those institutions contemplating the founding of such scholarly publishing departments, whether to profit by the account of Toronto's mistakes, or to be cheered by knowledge of such success as Toronto has enjoyed. It may also help to explain to some of those directly concerned with the founding of such presses, and to the general public, what university press publishing is about.

Then, too, although histories of world-famous publishing houses are not rare, comparatively little has been issued about publishing in Canada, and very little indeed about scholarly publishing in this country. This volume may, therefore, make a modest contribution to the economic and cultural history of the last sixty years in Canada.

It is hoped further that this account of one of the departments of the University of Toronto may be of interest to its faculty and alumni of today, and useful to its historians of tomorrow. While no one who participated in the founding of the Press remains, the years of service of those who have contributed to this volume add to an impressive total, and span more than one era in the development of the Press and of the University.

This book is also to a considerable degree an outgrowth of the articles which have been published during the past two years in the Press's house organ, *Press Notes*. The many expressions of interest the Press has received regarding such factual articles about its various operations seemed to indicate that the reproduction of a selection of this material in book form, together with added information, might not be unwelcome.

The editor wishes to thank most warmly the members of staff, who despite their preoccupation with regular responsibilities, found time to prepare their individual contributions. She is indebted to the Director of the Press, Mr. Marsh Jeanneret, for suggesting that the book be written, and for making its preparation and publication possible; and, further, for the use of his paper on "The University as Publisher," originally delivered as one of the New Foundation Lectures at McGill University.

E.H.

Contents

The
University
as
Publisher

The University as Publisher

Marsh Jeanneret

The purposes and possibilities of the scholarly publishing arm of any university are most easily perceived by those who comprehend the purposes of the university itself. Certainly one of the more subtle challenges faced by every academic administration today is the maintenance of the delicate balance that should exist between the institution's teaching functions and its research activities. Thus if our universities' responsibility for research, in the full meaning of that word, is imperfectly understood by the public, the responsibility for publishing the results of that research is even less likely to be grasped.

Canadians have shared the world-wide tendency to assume that every field of community service should be treated as a responsibility of government, perhaps even as a prerogative of government—municipal, provincial, or federal. Our society admits, of course, that some national services require administration by non-political bodies, even when these are assigned wholly or partly to the government for financial support. Unfortunately, the degree of freedom necessary for the health of such bodies as the Canadian Broadcasting Corporation and the Bank of Canada, to name two federal examples, is too frequently a matter of public controversy, even of political debate. It is conceivable, however, that the emancipation of public institutions from political control has been most successful in the case of our universities, and that through the creation of what is ordinarily described as academic freedom Western democracy may have made its greatest administrative achievement. At all events, the importance of academic freedom as a condition of objective scholarly research cannot be over-stated. When Disraeli remarked that "the university should be a place of light, liberty, and of learning," he was merely repeating the same idea for the sake of emphasis, for the important ingredient in this definition is liberty.

The unique feature of a university press publishing organization is that it provides scope for the free exercise of this scholarly objectivity. Because an academic author's freedom of expression is always in danger of being restricted, it may be worth while to consider briefly *why* a university press may be a surer guarantee of this freedom than any other channel of publishing.

A scholarly author's primary audience is normally his fellow-researchers in his own field of study. He may, therefore, avoid in his writing the exhaustive documentation of the obvious, an exercise which can be legitimate, or even necessary, in a post-graduate thesis. But he will be quick to support his premises with suitable editorial apparatus wherever his academic readers can be expected to question them, or deserve the privilege of weighing the sources used. His scholarly objectivity may thus affect his style, even to the point of limiting popular interest in a fashion that a commercial publisher would find totally disheartening. If commercial publication is thus denied an academic writer unless he is willing to compromise his treatment, will publication through a governmental department provide a satisfactory solution? I doubt this, for reasons which will follow, even though publication under governmental auspices is undoubtedly responsible today for dissemination of much important information.

Governmental publication, whether provincial or federal, can at least ensure availability of the results of research. But without denying the worth of many governmental publications, it can be asserted that true academic objectivity is less likely to flourish in government-sponsored bulletins and journals, just as full academic freedom is difficult to preserve within government departments. Every academic research programme, in every field, must be embarked upon with the intention of allowing the chips to fall where they may. Government publishing policy can seldom be freed of the question, asked in advance: "Where will the chips fall?" Admittedly, political expediency is least likely to be an issue in reports of scientific research, and in this regard the record of our National Research Council is an enviable one. But one may seriously question whether sociological research studies, to use a different example, can be expected from the Department of Labour unmarred by the suggestion that the information they contain is at least acceptable, politically speaking. What is directly sponsored by the public is normally calculated to please the public, or at least not to disquiet it. Comment that reflects upon the administration of a government department cannot be expected to be published by a government. How many economists fifteen years hence will be satisfied to trace the history of the Bank of Canada controversy of 1961 exclusively through official government publications? Or the history of Canada's trade policy vis-à-vis Cuba in 1960–61? Obviously, there must be a medium for responsible but independent writing about such matters, and that medium is much more likely to be a scholarly book or monograph published by a university press, or an article in the *Canadian Journal of Economics and Political Science*, than it is to be a brochure from a government printing bureau. This can be said notwithstanding the fact that the appointment as Queen's Printer of so distinguished a literary figure as Roger Duhamel promises a more creative approach to publishing by that department in the future.

Thus the needs of a scholarly author cannot always be served by governmental publication on the one hand, or by the commercial publisher on the other. The governmental publishing problem is a political one. The commercial publisher's difficulty is almost certain to be mainly economic, sometimes because of the scholar's specialized style, more often because of his specialized subject. This economic problem is felt with particular severity in Canada, where the comparatively small population and the unbookish North American tradition restrict the market severely. Thus it is necessary to subsidize publication in Canada of a considerable number of manuscripts, even including a few of a type that might attain commercial publication elsewhere. Nevertheless, one must pay tribute to the imaginative and often completely unselfish publishing services that have already been rendered by such great Canadian imprints as Macmillan of Canada, Ryerson Press, McClelland & Stewart, Clarke, Irwin, and others of their kind. It is to be hoped that these houses will do more, rather than less, academic publishing in the future, even though Canadian universities are already heavily in their debt. (It is equally true that the publication of Canadian literature in poetry and drama continues to be supported at a net over-all loss by these same Canadian commercial publishers, who must make ends meet by the sale of text-books and imported books.)

When considering the kinds of contemporary publishing that will be available to researchers in the future, it is important to note as well today's outpouring of serious journalistic comment, admittedly of varying degrees of excellence. But even though journalism today can be a useful recreation for the serious scholar, it cannot serve as a substitute for scholarly publishing. The reason for this distinction can be readily observed by considering the answers to such questions as, Why was this journalistic contribution written? To whom was it actually addressed? Why was it published? How was its success measured?

In short, the limitations on commercial publishing, governmental publishing, and journalism are not grounds for the wholesale condemnation of any of them as media for the dissemination of some scholarly research. Some of these publishing services inform readers innocuously; some of them interest readers informatively. But there is a residual requirement for a quite different medium of publication, with a quite different approach and purpose. There is a need for a medium that is not dependent on votes, on sales of editions, or on advertising circulation figures. Such a medium is the university press.

Although a scholarly press can occasionally discharge a useful function in other fields than the publishing of academic research, it must also be admitted that there are functions which a learned press is not so well designed to perform. These tabus can never be rigid, but must be permitted to vary with time and place. However, certain limitations are obvious, and others at least deserve consideration—if only to secure a better perspective of the several kinds of publishing that make up a national literature.

A distinction between academic writing and journalism as such has already been suggested; it is an important distinction, because scholars engage in both. At its best, journalism is concerned with the processing of existing knowledge; scholarship always seeks to add to the store. The success of journalism will in the end be measured quantitatively, if not in terms of circulation figures, then in terms of satisfaction of the readers. Scholarship will be evaluated qualitatively, and by other scholars. Journalism will always seek to create its own kind of impact; academic writing is not concerned with impact, at least not with impact for its own sake. Journalism is frequently aimed at the emotions of its readers; true scholarship distrusts mere emotionalism.

Distinctive features of journalistic writing such as these (to which others could be added) are important to a university press not as grounds for always rejecting such writing, but for the purpose of recognizing it when it occurs under the disguise of scholarly writing. This will probably happen most frequently in the social sciences, and a university press editor does well to be on the alert for it. But it is only when journalistic techniques adulterate scholarship that the former are dangerous. A book-length product of journalistic writing may well deserve publication by a learned press, and reading by academic readers. Nor should one underrate the extremely valuable contribution which is often made by a scholar who writes a popular yet soundly scientific exposition of his subject, and thus helps to bridge the gap between scholarly research and the general reader. This kind of writing may be entirely appropriate for publication by a university press; it certainly deserves publication. To the extent, however, that the subject-matter has an appeal sufficiently broad to make it acceptable to a commercial publisher, it is not the kind of publishing that a university press is uniquely fitted to make possible.

It need scarcely be added that in university press publishing there is not often a place for work by an amateur, just as there is not often a place in a graduate school for an untrained student. The imprint of a university press implies that the author has the necessary academic background to justify his undertaking academic research. (Every scholarly publisher can count an astonishing number of amateur economists, philosophers, and theologians ranging at large on this continent, and the amazing number of words committed to paper by them, most of which are in due course hopefully submitted to a university press!) But again the rules are not rigid, and the only definitive works that have been published recently on the North American buffalo and the early history of Canadian aviation did come to the University of Toronto Press from laymen. However, the same press has had to decline its share of outlines of new monetary systems, exposés of private enterprise, and Revelations of Revelations.

It has generally been held that a university press cannot provide its greatest service to book publishing in the field of fiction, or by issuing text-books below what is clearly the academic level. On the whole, these are reasonable restrictions on a learned press's activities, if only because authors of fiction can be better served by a commercial publisher, and because an elementary text-book programme would alter the character of a university press organization too drastically. This is not to say that useful experimental publishing cannot be done by a learned press in any field, but it would be best that the results of such experimentation be exploited by commercial publishers equipped to do so, lest commercial preoccupations distract a university press from its special duties.

Notwithstanding such limitations, and the exceptions to them, it would be as serious an error to suppose that successful publishing should never boast a university press imprint, as it would be to suggest that every unsaleable manuscript is a proper project for a scholarly press. Although the distinction is indeed often an economic one, it need not always be. To urge that unsaleability should be the only criterion for acceptance by a university press is to fail to recognize the basic fact that the planning of publications is itself normally a creative act, and that the execution of many publishing decisions requires an editorial contribution by the publisher second in importance only to that of the author. There is an endless list of creative projects whose realization demands much more from the publisher than the use of his imprint—the anthology of Canadian art, the special collection of articles by Soviet scholars on Russian education today, the aesthetic survey of Indian handicrafts, or the production of an anthology of photographic portraits made possible by a breakthrough in the graphic arts. Canadian literature would be the poorer, and Canadian publishing no richer, if the encouragement of such projects by university press publishers were stinted in any degree.

There are other limitations on the activities of a university press to which its administration must remain constantly alert. If any cynicism remains today regarding "deficit" scholarly publishing, it may be because of a lingering confusion between academic publishing and academic prestige. Scholarly publication is not a reward for effort expended, however noble that effort. Even our academic colleagues must occasionally be reminded that publication by a university press should occur for the benefit of scholarship, never merely to prove that it exists. A university wisely dedicates itself to the scholarly pursuit of knowledge for its own sake, but a university press must unmask every request for publication for its own sake, for the latter is indefensible.

A university press should strive to be no more parochial in its interests than is its parent institution, although this is not to say that the special reputation of a university in certain fields may not be reflected in its publishing programme. What must be preserved, however, is a complete editorial objectivity concerning the quality of the manuscripts accepted for publication. This objectivity can best be ensured by bringing to the editorial committee the most authoritative and most detached readers' reports that can be procured. It follows that these reports will normally be from other institutions than the author's own, that the reader's anonymity will be scrupulously protected by the university press and by the editorial committee, and—most important, perhaps—that care will have been taken to procure a quality of reports which will permit the editorial committee to make a sound decision. A press's greatest responsibilities probably arise in connection with the procuring and administration of these readers' reports.

A university press does much more than disseminate the results of scholarly investigation, important though that function is. It increases enormously the academic effectiveness of scholars whose works it publishes, and of scholars who see in it the prospect for publication of work on which they are engaged. Thus the learned press becomes a powerful catalyst in the programmes of research, at its own institution particularly, but to a considerable extent at other centres as well. Of all the many ways in which a university endeavours to create the ideal environment for a community of scholars, what more effective stimulus can it supply than the assurance that its scholars will be enabled to communicate effectively with their colleagues at large? More than this, the books and journals that emanate from a university press are instruments for scholarly communication and information not only today, but for all time. The availability of a scholarly publishing facility, sensibly administered and sensitive to its great responsibilities, can be as important an academic feature on any campus as a new lecture hall or a new administration building, although the latter may require many times the capital investment.

Scholarship recognizes standards that are international; the standards of scholarly publishing must also be international. But the concerns of scholarship are no more identical throughout the world than is the priority of subjects for scholarly investigation. The spontaneous development in the United States of more than fifty learned presses, and of the several scholarly imprints in the United Kingdom, possesses a special significance for institutions of higher learning in Canada. If certain areas of study in this country are to be explored adequately, the necessary research must also be nurtured in this country, granted that such research must never be regimented.

Academic investigations in the Canadian social sciences— including history, economics, political science, and law—as well as in Canadian literature itself, are unlikely to be reported in either adequate or timely fashion by foreign learned presses. This is not to say that such Canadian studies will be ignored abroad, if they are made accessible to foreign scholars working in parallel but not identical fields. But this accessibility is a condition of their complete recognition, and can only be ensured if there is a strong university press publishing tradition within this country.

Through the full flowering here of such a learned press tradition, our domestic scholarship will be served not only in

Canadian literature and the Canadian social sciences, but in many other academic areas as well. Scholarly investigation in the fields just named would obviously be stifled if Canada were to lack university press publishing facilities in sufficient measure; the reporting of research in other disciplines can also be enormously stimulated by the proximity of a strong network of effective university presses in Canada. Canadian research in the Romance languages, in philosophy, in mathematics, and in the natural sciences will be vastly encouraged by the knowledge that prompt and effective publication is available to competent work, and that academic quality rather than commercial feasibility will determine the treatment to be accorded the finished manuscript. Research in the great professions will also be better served by the existence within our country of a stronger university press tradition, and it is worth asserting that such a tradition will be enriched if it is fostered by several academic institutions, rather than by one, or for that matter, even by two.

Although the responsibilities of a university press may be imperfectly understood by the general public, the importance of their being comprehended perfectly by those most closely associated with the press should be obvious. If such a thing as institutional expediency, for example, really does exist outside the minds of narrow men, it can never colour university press publishing policy. It is quite possibly true that institutional expediency has never influenced a single publishing decision in university press publishing in this country. University of Toronto Press journals publish, with discomforting frequency, reviews criticizing harshly but honestly the publications issued over the same imprint. In the future, it is to be hoped, the publications of several Canadian scholarly presses will sometimes find favour and will sometimes be found wanting in each other's eyes, and Canadian scholarship will benefit from the academic detachment that will characterize the findings by each.

Uncompromising scholarly integrity will govern the relations among Canadian university presses in the future just as it has enriched the relations among all learned presses in the past. This quality of integrity will be derived chiefly from the members of the editorial committee of the faculty on whom rests the final responsibility for selection and rejection of manuscripts, or at least of those manuscripts requiring publishing subsidies. It is an integrity that must be of the pure, unadulterated, academic kind, for the whole policy of a university press flows from it, and from nowhere else. The interests of the press will in the long run be the interests of the parent academic community; through

Canada's university presses scholars will be conversing with scholars, and always on a scholarly, not an institutional, basis.

The university press as publisher does not necessarily imply the university press as printer, and, indeed, only seven of the fifty members of the Association of American University Presses control their own manufacturing facilities. While a university may through its printing plant service its own departments efficiently, and possibly take some lead in the development of the graphic arts, the publishing activities of the university, if pursued vigorously, tend to expand beyond the capacities of the university printing plant. Thus one finds at Oxford, at Cambridge, at Chicago, at California, and also at Toronto, that a very large proportion of the publications of the university press are produced in printing plants other than those on campus. Columbia University Press, which publishes a formidable list of books each year, has no plant investment or responsibilities at all, and Columbia provides the norm rather than the exception.

Nonetheless, university press books in America, whether produced in a university's own plant, or by a commercial book manufacturer, do have attributes (in addition to their textual content) which give them a distinctive character. The outstanding feature of a university press book is probably the thoroughness of the editorial preparation accorded the manuscript before printing. In the editorial department, the author is given the privilege of a painstaking and conscientious examination of his manuscript by an editor who is accustomed by long training to handling complex scholarly material. This editor, if not actually a specialist in the same field as the author, normally holds a good honours degree in an allied discipline, and is deeply sympathetic to the author's scholarly aims. His or her purpose is to assist in the communication of the author's ideas, not to substitute other ideas for them, and to suggest the removal of ambiguities or obscurities or awkwardnesses, not to destroy the author's original wording. The degree of assistance given to the author will, of course, depend on the state of the manuscript when it arrives in the editorial office. Some manuscripts require more exhaustive editorial consultation than others, although it does not follow that the intrinsic worth of the book varies inversely with the amount of editing it requires. A gifted editor may be able to inspire an author so to revise his manuscript that it reaches unanticipated heights. But whether much editorial assistance is needed or little, a university press is prepared to expend upon a given manuscript an amount of care that would normally be quite uneconomic in a commercial house.

University presses, too, have long placed great emphasis on the typographical design and the quality of production of their books. This is as it should be, for these are not volumes that are read in the thousands for a year or two and then tossed into discard. Instead, they stand in libraries and on reference shelves year after year, a continuing witness to the fine taste, or the bad judgment, of their designers and their publishers. They are made of durable materials, for they are meant to last. At the present moment, for example, a pioneer experiment is under way with acid-free book-papers designed to last far beyond the usual 50-year life of book-papers generally produced today, and university presses are taking a leading part in this graphic arts research programme.

While occasionally commercial publishers have been known to comment with some jealousy on the physical quality of university press books, pointing out that such emphasis on production is uneconomic, the actual fact is that university publishers have been driven by scarcity of funds to the careful planning that often distinguishes their product. When resources are limited, every dollar must be made to count. University publishers have found that good, not elaborate, design and complete pre-planning may save rather than cost them money, especially in the short-run editions to which they are accustomed.

Sometimes the observation is made—not so often nowadays—that university press books, while generally dignified and impressive, may be somewhat stodgy in appearance. This is not, in my opinion, a fair comment. It is not necessary, in fact it is not desirable, to make a serious academic work resemble a best-seller. A flashy, inappropriate format cheapens the seriousness of the author's intention and may give the work an air of ephemerality which it does not deserve.

The same special care and planning that are given to the editing and production of a university press book must necessarily be accorded the promotion of its sale. A university press publication seldom if ever can be promoted in a routine way, and only very rarely by a Madison Avenue formula. Each book is written for a particular market, and however small or obscure that market may be, it must be searched out and advised of the publication of the book. To achieve this, a university press undertakes a kind of detailed promotion that would often seem unreasonable to a large trade publisher. Indeed, such promotion can be relatively costly. Direct mail distribution of prospectuses, one of the chief methods used by a university press to acquaint scholars with the availability of its products, is (contrary to the frequent impression) one of the most expensive ways of selling books. It is far less expensive to engage salesmen to sell books in bulk directly to bookstores, when that can be done. However, university presses do not publish novels, and usually only a small proportion of their books are popular enough to warrant their being stocked heavily by bookstores. In North America, at least, methods to supplement direct representation by salesmen must be used to reach the special public interested; it is the costly method of direct mail advertising that is generally used to hunt down readers individually.

The distribution of its books to foreign users provides another interesting challenge to a university press. The world of scholarship has no borders, either of geography or of language, and many of the products of Canadian research are read by students in every part of the world. To reach these scholars, agents may be engaged in many different countries abroad; editions may be sold to publishers located in Great Britain, France, Holland, the United States, India, Australia, or elsewhere. One day a university press publisher will receive a request for translation rights from Poland; or the next from Tokyo. These editions and sales of rights do not ordinarily produce high returns in zlotys and yen (and the rubles from pirated editions are nil), but its university's contribution to scholarship becomes world-wide. Surely it is a pardonable ambition for a university press to seek the recognition of its imprint by every learned institution in the world.

It is perhaps no more realistic to suppose that a scholarly publishing programme can be supported without net cost to the parent institution than it is to suggest that an academic department should justify its existence simply by a profit and loss statement. But the importance of realistic accounting in the publishing department should not be diminished by this comparison. Methods of accounting do, of course, vary widely among the universities that support presses, but it must be recognized that a programme of subsidizing that is expected to return through sales all costs of operation is not a programme of subsidizing at all; at best it would imply financing, and presumably financing of a kind that could be better undertaken by a commercial publisher. There is some importance to be attached to this distinction, because there are presses that operate under institutional pressures that not only distract them from their chief function, but that also cause them to account for their costs of operation in ways which are not in the best interests of their own continued growth and development.

Although such unrealistic accounting methods are normally not initiated by a press so much as by the institution itself, they can at times amount to well-intentioned concealment of the true costs of the publishing operation. There are various forms which such concealment may take. The salaries of the chief officers, or of the editorial staff, may appear in the academic or administrative budget of the university rather than in the operating statements of the press. Mailing costs may be treated as part of general university expenditures, or costs of office space and maintenance may not be reflected in the press's accounting. It is very true that such practices may begin as well-meant and generous forms of support to a scholarly publishing activity. But in so far as some of the areas indirectly assisted in this way may represent fluctuating overhead costs—costs that must increase with growth, for example—the press's very ability to expand will embarrass the generosity that brought it into being, and which often cannot keep pace with the growing needs of an otherwise flourishing publishing department. The difficulty can be avoided by adding the true value of such indirect subsidies to the official support given to the press, which will then have a sound basis for planning its future capacities and development.

Every administrative service in a university institution should be truthfully costed and correctly charged—whether or not the department being serviced must receive a corresponding increase in its annual grant. The moment that services are supplied at below true cost, for example on the argument that "the staff and equipment are there anyway," some degree of Parkinsonism will set in. It is regrettably true that unjustifiable comparisons may be made between true costs from one department and the partially subsidized costs from another—even for the same class of service. When this happens, the administrative error in policy will expose itself in due course. Such false costing must be avoided, by a university press especially, even if embarrassing comparisons with the so-called "costs" of other departments from time to time may thereby be invited. These other departments will not long survive the criticism that they will receive, from good accountants, as they advertise their services. The practice of basing all charges on true costs is as valid for an institution such as Toronto—where the Press is authorized to divert net income from its various operations to the subsidizing of scholarly publications—as it is for presses whose subsidies are provided directly by the parent institution. This is probably the most important single consideration in the administrative structure of a university press.

It is therefore important for a university to know exactly how much it spends on its subsidized publishing programme, and it is even more important for it to be able to measure and plan the future development of such a programme. The publishing budget should be a source of institutional satisfaction, and the situation should be avoided where, as a result of increased publishing activity, it might for no clear reason come to be disparaged. Quite unlike any other university department, a university press can be embarrassed by reason of the fact that it handles money but does not make money. The fact that commercial publishing is profitable seems to cast a reflection on the university publishing operation which is not profitable, and which could be a commercial success only by transforming itself into something other than what it was designed to be.

The function of its university press, then, is big enough and important enough for a university to add up every cent of the true annual cost of this department, present the figures proudly in the institution's Annual Report, and—if the quality and quantity of the scholarly writing justify it—to increase the budget in the following year. To be willing to do this, however, the university administration must possess unreserved confidence in the accounting system of the press. This accounting system must make plain that this uncommercial enterprise is being run with strictly commercial efficiency; and that the so-called losses of the press are incurred according to budget. What these losses produce in scholarly books and journals, well edited, attractively produced, and imaginatively merchandised, constitutes the true measure of the success of the scholarly press. The late Sidney Smith always deplored these costs being referred to as deficits, preferring to speak of the books and the journals as the "dividends" on the investment. There is much to be said in favour of such an interpretation.

It might also be observed here that the publishing department of a university invites a larger flow of inexpert criticism than does any other department within the institution, or any business outside it. This is certainly an interesting phenomenon. It can perhaps be explained partly by the fact that publishing, like bookselling, is still some distance from full maturity on this continent. It is also to be admitted that publishing is, after all, the most fascinating of all enterprises to the bibliophile, who happily is everywhere in an academic community. In short, a press administration should realize that advice from its constituents is to be vastly preferred to their indifference, and that the challenge is to learn how to make the best possible use of the ideas and suggestions that will flow in from everywhere, while at the same time seeking to encourage more.

It is not, of course, beyond the realm of possibility that some of the cost of supporting or expanding a university press may be borne by others than the university administration itself. Two North American scholarly presses have been bequeathed profitable commercial enterprises, and one inherited a magnificent printing plant. Yale's new press building, opened just recently, was made possible by the contributions of alumni, who responded from every corner of the continent to a special campaign on its behalf. Toronto was recently joined by Les Presses de l'Université Laval in the planning of the *Dictionary of Canadian Biography/ Dictionnaire Biographique du Canada*, made possible by one of the most remarkable bequests in publishing history anywhere, when the late James Nicholson left a capital sum now valued at more than a million and a quarter dollars for this specific project. The benefits of philanthropy will be felt by Canadian university presses, present as well as future, perhaps to finance the editing and publication of major Canadian projects not yet planned, but which will confer honour, and taxation benefits, upon the philanthropist, and still greater academic prestige upon the institutions concerned.

In conclusion it is to be noted that, while regional publishing—interpreted narrowly or broadly—is frequently characteristic of university press publishing, Canadian university presses should strive to publish a wide variety of manuscripts from many sources, academic as well as non-academic, from authors on-campus and off-campus. As other Canadian university presses join McGill, Laval, and Toronto, each press will also develop its own special fields, and if this happens it will be natural for manuscripts in such specialties to gravitate to the institution which features them. Canadian scholarship everywhere will benefit by the growth of university press publishing in this country. A friendly but intelligent jealousy regarding publishing accomplishments among Canadian university presses of the future may even be a commendable condition. It would be a disheartening thought for Canadian literature if there should never be cause for such mutual compliments. But there need never be jealousy among presses regarding the privilege of subsidizing scholarly publishing, because the resources of all bodies that expend funds in this direction—including the Canada Council, various learned councils and foundations, universities, and other institutions—are still far from adequate to meet the requirements. Indeed, the need for such support in this country is only too likely to outstrip the resources, as scholarship burgeons alongside academic facilities and university enrolments.

It is hardly necessary to add that the net annual financial cost of a scholarly publishing programme should always be a source of pride to a university, representing as it does an expenditure on the final stage of research. If a university press's status on its own campus is ever limited to that of a purely administrative, service, or clerical department, whatever assistance it may render to the academic branch will all too likely be measured as an administrative financial deficit and nothing more. But so long as university presses and parent universities in this country perceive that their purposes are identical, Canadian research will be stimulated in every field, and the interests of our future scholarship will be well served.

Founding a University Press

Eleanor Harman

The foundations of the University of Toronto Press were laid during the academic year 1901–2, and it published its first book in 1911. The year 1961 therefore marks the golden anniversary of its book publishing career, as well as the diamond anniversary of its service to the University.

In the autumn of 1901, the Standing Committee of the Senate on Printing considered the matter of University printing, and more particularly the production of examination papers and the University calendar. The firm which had been doing University printing had gone out of business, and tenders were asked from four Toronto firms on University work; at the same time inquiries were initiated regarding the advisability of establishing a University printing office. The Committee consulted "a number of experts," including John Ross Robertson, E. F. Clarke, M.P., and James Bain. Their opinion was unanimous in favour of establishing a printing office, and in its report the Committee added the recommendation that a Linotype machine should not be purchased, and that type should be set by hand. This report was not formally presented to the Board of Trustees of the University until January 30, 1902. The Minutes of the Board of Trustees for that date state:

> As a first step toward carrying out this plan it is recommended that the services of a first class practical printer be obtained at a salary of $10 or $15 a week who[se] first duty it would be to advise as to the plant to be purchased. The initial cost will not exceed $1,000. With this plant and the hiring of a few compositors for about four weeks the composition and press work of the examination papers and class lists together with the composition of the calendar could all be done at the University, the press work and binding of the Calendar being done elsewhere.

In recommending the above plan the Committee desires to emphasize the advantage in enabling confidential work like examination papers to be done on the premises. At the same time the Committee believes that not only will the cost of printing the examination papers and calendar be reduced, but much miscellaneous printing required but hitherto not undertaken for want of money, may also be done at a trifling cost, whilst other work, such as the printing of the "University Monthly" and "Studies" may be undertaken at a profit.

Two small presses and a stock of type were purchased, and the University Press was installed in a room of the old Wycliffe College Building, which at the time was standing vacant at the head of McCaul Street. Some months later, the administration decided to tear down the Wycliffe College Building in order to construct the Mining Building, and President Loudon on behalf of the Press applied to the Acting Director of the Observatory "and obtained from him possession of the rough-cast cottage on the Observatory grounds on condition of providing a house for the messenger." This house was located behind the present Convocation Hall. (A later Minute records ruefully that the alterations required, which had been estimated at $300, actually came to $554.) In these modest quarters, the Press continued its limited operations until 1910. All typesetting was done by hand, or by purchase of machine composition from trade houses in the city.

In 1904, Mr. R. J. Hamilton, manager of the Students' Book Department, was appointed book-keeper to the Press. The Students' Book Department had been begun in 1897 by Miss McMicking, a member of the staff of the University Library. She was given permission to sell books to students when she was not on duty in the Library, and was permitted to keep her stock of books in the basement of the Library building. The volume of book sales grew very rapidly, and when Miss McMicking's health made it necessary for her to give up the enterprise, the Book Department was taken over by Mr. Hamilton in 1904 as a private business under an agreement made with the Library Committee of the University.

Following the establishment of the Printing Committee by the Board of Governors in 1906, Mr. Hamilton was appointed secretary, and a year later became manager of the Press. Since the Students' Book Department was already located in the Library, it followed rather naturally that when the Library was enlarged in 1910, the Press was also moved to the basement of the Library. There was soon a complaint about the chattering of the Monotype caster and the rumbling of the presses disturbing readers, and their location was changed to another part of the basement. Both the Press and the Students' Book Department remained in the Library until 1920. The productive capacity of the Press had been greatly enlarged by the addition of the Mono-type keyboard and caster, a cylinder press, and several items of bindery equipment—the rebinding of books for the Library now becoming an important part of the Press's activities.

The Press soon began to manufacture, in addition to calendars and examination papers, a number of manuals for members of the Faculty. These were financed by the professors themselves, as the Press at this time was not undertaking publishing ventures of its own. In February of 1911, the new Monotype was reported as "running day and night, with two sets of operators." The necessity for proofreading became apparent, but "rather than employing a permanent Proof Reader who would be idle part of his time, the Committee approved of the employment of two regular clerks in the Book Department during their spare time by piecework at the lowest prevailing rate." Another notation in the Minutes of the Printing Committee Meeting has a familiar ring: "In consequence of the great delay, the inconvenience caused, and the additional expense, in publishing the Calendar of the University this year, the Secretary was instructed to write to the Senate respectfully requesting that body to bring before the various Faculty Councils the necessity of having the copy for the Calendar ready for the printer not later than January 15th of each year." *Plus ça change* . . . .

Under Mr. Hamilton's managership, both the Students' Book Department and the University Press prospered, although clouds at times arose on the horizon. In 1905, the Ontario Government received a protest from retail booksellers in Toronto concerning the operations of the Students' Book Department, but Mr. Hamilton was able to produce evidence that no off-campus sales were sought; in fact a sign posted in the Department indicated that customers who were not students or members of the Faculty should take their business elsewhere. Relations between the Press bindery and its host, the Library, were not always of the happiest; within two years of the establishment of the bindery, the problem of the price at which rebindings were to be charged arose; in 1915 and in 1916, the matter came up again, with the Librarian claiming that he could purchase better and cheaper re-bindings in England and the Press manager pointing out that the specifications in each case were different. In 1919, trouble arose over the length of time taken by the Press for rebindings, and this was attributed by the manager to the inadequacy of bindery staff—presumably because of the shortage of employees during World War I. (Some of these difficulties may have been caused by the fact that the first foreman of the bindery, a capable and experienced binder, was also of a somewhat inflexible disposition, as those who knew him in later years will attest.) An argument arose as to whether the Bindery Department of the Press had been specifically established to handle the Library rebindings, which should, therefore, be given precedence over other work, but an appeal to the Bursar on this ground did not find supporting evidence in the records of the University.

The printing business of the University was prospering steadily, and the question whether the Press might not begin to publish on its own account began to be discussed. The first book produced in the Press, dated 1911, was a study of Sir James Gowan (a pioneer senator and judge) but this was for private distribution and was paid for by friends of the subject of the biography. The second book to come off the presses was entitled *A Short Handbook of Latin Accidence and Syntax* (1912), and was written by Professor J. Fletcher, Head of the Department of Classics in University College. This was a text-book for university use, and appears to have been the first actual publishing venture of the Press.

In the meantime, the publishing programme of the University was progressing under other auspices. In 1897, the University of Toronto Studies had been begun by resolutions of the combined Faculties of the University, University College, Victoria University, and the School of Practical Science. A Committee of Management to control the Studies was appointed, the first General Editor being H. H. Langton, the University Librarian. His budget consisted of a grant from the Minister of Education for Ontario, which amounted to $1,000 in 1898, and a grant of $300 from the Library Committee in return for the use of the Studies as exchange items. The government grant, however, was in the form of a credit for printing to be done by the Queen's Printer, and when the Committee demonstrated that it could secure more printing for the same money by letting the contracts itself, the grant was promptly reduced to $500 in cash.

At the outset, the Studies consisted partly of reprints of papers by members of the University which had appeared in the *Transactions of the Canadian Institute* (now the Royal Canadian Institute), and elsewhere, and partly of original papers. Year by year, the Studies were enlarged, to include series in natural science, physical science, mathematical science, psychology, philosophy, history and economics, and philology. One of the main expenditures of the Studies Committee was on the publication of the *Review of Historical Publications Relating to Canada*, founded in 1896, which later developed into the *Canadian Historical Review* (1920).

In 1918, a proposal to establish a publishing programme at the University of Toronto Press was put forward by Mr. Hamilton. (The name of the Press had been changed from The University Press in 1915.) The Printing Committee, in making its recommendation to the Board of Governors, held that "if proper care is taken in the selection of manuscripts and the mechanical work [is] well done, it will be a source of revenue." The Board of Governors was sympathetic, but felt that inquiries should be made, whereupon the manager of the Press wrote to university presses at Chicago, Yale, Princeton, Johns Hopkins, and Harvard to ask: "1. The way they control or make their selection of books, and their relation to the University. 2. How they are financed. 3. How much they spend on Publication which can never become remunerative." The replies were evidently satisfactory, for in March of 1919, the Board of Governors authorized establishment of a publishing department, with the rider, however, that its debit must at no time exceed $2,000. The Committee "considered this quite satisfactory for the present and felt that an important step in advance had been made by the Press." The intention, however, was not to subsidize publication, for each manuscript, in addition to being reported on favourably by a committee of three, had to be approved by the Printing Committee as "a good business proposition from a financial point of view." Presumably, the programme of the Studies Committee was felt to be adequate provision for subsidized publishing by the University as a whole.

Since the Press at this time was showing a substantial annual profit on its manufacturing operations, the plan of embarking in a modest way on a broader book publishing programme was a natural step. In view of the history of Canadian publishing during the following four decades, it can also be described as optimistic. There was money to be made at that time in publishing in Canada, but it was to be made in the publishing of authorized text-books for use in elementary and secondary schools, and not in general publishing, especially of an academic kind. Hugh Eayrs, President of Macmillan of Canada during the twenties and thirties, who conducted an active programme of general Canadian publishing, maintained that the publishing by his firm of Canadian books apart from text-books showed a net loss. Such views prevailed in Canadian publishing, at least up to World War II. Nevertheless a limited number of Canadian publishers did handle fiction and popular biography, together with a much smaller number of what might be regarded as "academic" books. Mr. Hamilton doubtless anticipated publishing at a profit text-books for use in the University, but it is doubtful if he appreciated the actual overhead costs of a publishing programme. Indeed, text-books produced for professors were at one time sold by the Press on 10 per cent commission, and in one case at least, on 5 per cent. While sums were appropriated annually for the purchase of new plant equipment, there existed no regular plan for depreciating the value of equipment already purchased, nor a programme for constant renewal of the plant; if such provision had been made, the annual "profit" might not have loomed so large.

The Press had indeed accumulated sufficient surplus on its operations that when new quarters were needed, it was able to finance their construction. By 1920, the Library required for its own use the basement area occupied by the Students' Book Department and by the Press, and the latter organizations also required more space for their activities.

The new site, which is still occupied by the manufacturing departments of the Press, was to the west of the Physics and Chemistry buildings of that era, and in the words of Professor John Squair, who contributed a brief article on the Press to the *University of Toronto Monthly* in 1920, it was a site "unsuitable for other purposes." It was, in fact, the location of the former dwelling of James Mavor, Professor of Economics. The new building was a storey and a half but was capable of subsequent enlargement, which actually took place only six years later when the second floor was completed and a third floor added. The Students' Book Department occupied a large area of the ground floor, as tenant. Professor Squair also comments, "Before leaving the old quarters in the Library, the Press, in addition to the annual charge for heat and light, had repaid all sums lent to it by the University, so that its plant to the value of over $40,000, was a real asset of the University. In addition, there was on June 30 last a sum of $16,000 of accumulated savings in the hands of the Bursar. Its policy has been to do all work for the University at the very lowest price possible, and to refuse all work which might come to it from the general public."

Shortly after the completion of the new building, the Press came under fire in the matter of its printing costs—possibly sparked by the complaints of the Library Committee about binding—and an investigation was made by the Toronto Typothetae (the organization of printers which preceded the Toronto Graphic Arts Council). To the gratification of the manager, the Typothetae reported, "The records thus far prove beyond any doubt that the University Press as pertaining to organization, character of work, quantity of work, morale of employees, and cost of production, compares most favourably with other similar plants, in fact, is much better than the average of Toronto." However, it was noted "the percentage [of Authors' Alterations] is abnormally high, and reflects a condition which detracts very materially from production in this department, which no doubt could be very greatly improved if proper care were taken in preparation of the original copy by the several authors." There did not, of course, at this time exist at the Press any editorial service or office, and the manuscripts proceeded direct from author to printer—as, indeed, they usually did in most publishing houses in Canada at the time. The Typothetae also cleared the University Press of charges of inefficiency in the operation of the bindery during 1914–19, and the Printing Committee noted that "our Committee is gratified to learn from the report made by the Typothetae that having regard for the conditions that prevailed in other binderies during the period, the University of Toronto Press has maintained such a high degree of efficiency."

An interesting production of the years following the establishment of the Press in new quarters was the two-volume, 1941-page *Transactions and Proceedings of the International Mathematical Congress*; this Congress met at Toronto in 1924. The large work, full of mathematical formulae and complex type-setting, was completed in 1928. In those days, of course, all of the formula matter was set by hand. The volumes were edited by Professor J. C. Fields, then Research Professor of Mathematics at the University. It was a remarkable achievement for a small printing house, even allowing for the several years spent on its production. The Press itself contributed substantially to the cost, making a grant of $2,000 towards the project (perhaps, it may be conjectured, because it had no prospect of collecting its bill).

In the next few years, the Press continued to issue a limited number of texts and manuals, a considerable number of which were paid for by the authors, and a few taken on at risk. The Publications account showed an annual loss until 1926–28 (in these three years, however, almost no publishing was done—perhaps compositors and equipment were tied up with the enormous International Mathematical Congress Proceedings); subsequently, the pattern of annual losses was resumed. However, the manufacturing department of the Press continued to prosper and to provide an annual net income; in 1929, $5,000 was transferred from surplus to assist the publication of the *Catalogue of Vases in the Royal Ontario Museum*, and a substantial amount still remained.

In 1927, the Committee had discussed ways of employing the surplus, and it seems most probable that it was this comparative affluence that led the Printing Committee to propose in 1929 that it should confer with the University Studies Committee about the possibility of an amalgamation for the purpose of carrying on the publications of the University. Agreement was reached, and the recommendation was duly made to the Board of Governors, which approved it. Both the University Studies Committee and the Printing Committee were superseded by a new University Committee on Printing and Publishing, which was given combined responsibility for the printing plant and the publishing programme of the University. Along with the trust funds of the University Studies Committee, the Press now inherited the financial responsibility for the *Canadian Historical Review*, which had become a quarterly in 1920.

The records do not show a clear formulation of policy at this time. The Press had a surplus which might logically be expended on publications, and obviously the intention was to so expend it. But there seems to have been no planning of editorial, design, and business departments, nor anticipation of the costs of operating such. While presumably it was not contemplated that the entire programme could be carried out at a profit, there was a failure to recognize that certain books would have to be taken on in the full expectation of a loss, and budgeted for accordingly. It may have been hoped that in time the profitable publications would balance the unprofitable ones, but as it was set up in 1929, the Publications Department was bound inevitably to become the Cinderella of the Press organization, a status it continued to enjoy for many years.

Some discussion took place about the appointment of a General Editor, but no decision was reached. In the interim, Mr. W. Stewart Wallace, Librarian of the University, formerly General Editor of the Studies, agreed to carry on. In May of 1932, Miss Alison Ewart (later Mrs. A. W. B. Hewitt) of the Library staff, who had been giving valuable assistance to the Editor of the *Canadian Historical Review* for some years, was appointed to the post of General Editor of all Press publications. Miss Ewart was an experienced and capable editor, who not only handled all publications that passed through her own hands with taste, skill, and discretion, but in the end trained a small but efficient staff to work under her. Her position was not entirely enviable; as the head of a "loss" department, she had to operate on an inadequate budget, and to maintain the integrity of the editorial office against, it must be said, the opposition of the manager, who, despite his general capabilities as a man of business, did not understand or appreciate the importance of what her office was doing, or why it should cost so much to do it. This attitude, let us concede, was shared by a number of other executives in Canadian publishing houses of the time, few of whom had any real conception of the editorial process.

In the same year that Miss Ewart became General Editor, Mr. A. Gordon Burns, who had been Secretary-Treasurer of the Students' Administrative Council, was appointed Assistant Manager of the Press. Some discussion occurred in 1932 about the advisability of the Press's taking over the Students' Book Department, and the amalgamation finally took place in 1933, when the University purchased Mr. Hamilton's financial interest in it. It was given the name of "The University of Toronto Press Book Department." Mr. Hamilton remained as manager, and was paid a salary by the Press for his services. In 1934, the Book Department employed a young law student as assistant, who was later to return to the Press at a different level—Mr. Marsh Jeanneret, the present Director. Mr. Jeanneret also devoted part of his time to collating note-books in the Press bindery.

Mr. Hamilton had been in charge of the combined printing, publishing, and bookstore operation under the aegis of the University for only three years when he died in 1936. Mr. Burns was appointed Acting Manager, and became Manager in 1938.

Meanwhile the Publications Department was expanding. In 1935 was published *A Catalogue of Books, Periodicals, and Studies Published by the University of Toronto Press*. The greater part of this first catalogue comprises the Studies (some four hundred items, many of which were small reprints), eighteen theses for the D.Paed. degree, and approximately one hundred and fifty School of Engineering Research Bulletins. It lists seventy "books"—some of which were, however, pamphlets. The periodicals are four—*The Canadian Historical Review, University of Toronto Quarterly, The University of Toronto Law Journal*, and *The Canadian Journal of Economics and Political Science*.

This extensive programme of journal publishing had been embarked on by the Press in the course of a very few years. As previously mentioned, the *Canadian Historical Review* came to the Press following the amalgamation with the University of Toronto Studies. In 1931, after much discussion, a journal of the humanities, the *University of Toronto Quarterly*, was begun. In 1934, the Press joined with the Canadian Political Science Association in beginning the *Canadian Journal of Economics and Political Science*, and founded the *University of Toronto Law Journal* on its own account, under the insistent prompting of Dean W. P. M. Kennedy. Nothing attests more fully to the optimism created by the Press surpluses than the shouldering, in such quick succession, of the main financial responsibility for these distinguished journals. The Press had, of course, no experience in the publishing of journals; it was probably not even fully aware of how much time had been given, at slight remuneration, to the *Canadian Historical Review* over the years by the editor, Mr. W. Stewart Wallace, and by Dr. George W. Brown, who served as assistant editor and succeeded Mr. Wallace as editor, or how much effort had been contributed by Miss Ewart and Miss J. Jarvis of the Library staff in preparing the articles for the printer. The cost of administering subscriptions and the difficulties in the way of securing advertising both appear to have been underestimated. And when embarking on this ambitious programme, no one, of course, had any idea that the University itself during the Depression would have to absorb into its general funds a major portion of the Press's accumulated surplus. This, of course, it had every right to do, as the Press was then constituted, but it would probably not have happened had the publications policy of the Press been established, nor might it have occurred if the Press had had an accounting system which provided adequately for depreciation and for renewal of equipment, thereby presenting more realistic surpluses.

As it was, publication costs of the journals steadily mounted, and as the financial pressure became heavier, many efforts were made to reduce cost, accompanied by an understandable amount of recrimination between the Press and the various academic editors. The latter were contributing time and effort far beyond the token editorial payments made to them by the Press, and were subjected to frequent appeals to reduce the number of pages, to use fewer varieties of type, and so on. In 1938 the Editorial Office became the centre of the storm. It was claimed that the volume of services given to the journals had increased so greatly over the years that the General Editor of the Press had virtually become the assistant editor of each of these periodicals.

A sub-committee, appointed to investigate the matter, brought in a recommendation that a cash allowance be made to each of the editors in lieu of the Press's editorial services. However, following representations from the journal editors, the matter was considered further. The merits of centralizing the preparation of copy in one office were noted, among them being the distribution of work over several persons to take care of peak loads, the maintenance of quality in the editing, and the avoidance of duplication of effort. Particular tribute was paid to the quality of the work done by Miss Ewart and her assistants; Professor Woodhouse, Editor of the *Quarterly*, said, "No one can receive Miss Ewart's aid without being grateful for it or without being sensible of her devoted and efficient service to the University." Professor Brown, Editor of the *Canadian Historical Review*, pointed out that the *Review* had actually received much more of Miss Ewart's time during the period before the Press took over the journal. Professor V. W. Bladen, Editor of the *Canadian Journal of Economics and Political Science*, wrote to the manager of the Press, "The proposal to disorganize an [editorial] office which has been built up over many years and which is functioning smoothly and efficiently is sufficiently disturbing to warrant a letter of this length. I may add that the harassing of editors as an annual sport in the University should stop."

This was not the first, nor indeed the last, time in the history of the Press that the "problem of the journals" came to the fore. The financing of an academic journal involves special problems, and it required many years and much accumulated experience for the Press to develop a policy to which it could adhere. Indeed, the variety of publishing arrangements under which the journals of the Press (now ten in number) are issued, despite modifications made by mutual consent of the parties concerned, constitute an historical commentary on the gradual development of a consistent policy regarding their publication.

At the same time, the contribution which the Press was making through its journals programme to the cause of Canadian scholarship during these years should not be minimized. Each of these journals was the sole medium for publishing the output of Canadian scholarship in its own field; before they started no such medium existed, and for many years afterwards (and indeed in some respects today) University of Toronto Press journals were and are the only outlet for scholarship of less than book length in this country. Difficult though it was for the Press to maintain them financially, their academic importance could not be overrated, and the Committee, the Associations, and the editors concerned were all fully aware of the essentiality of what was being done.

It should not be assumed, either, that the presence of the journals in the editorial office was in any sense holding back the publication of books. Books were certainly not being crowded out. Unless the manager of the Press discouraged many authors before they came to the point of presenting their works to the Committee (which seems highly improbable in the academic environment), book-length manuscripts were certainly not arriving before World War II in the numbers that came afterwards. Possibly, would-be authors did not receive sufficient encouragement, nor did they see sufficient possibility of publication, to induce them to complete their manuscripts. But the records indicate that the body of book manuscripts that were submitted received generous publishing treatment.

As mentioned, the Great Depression was presumably responsible for the decision of the University to absorb the Press's accumulated surplus. There is evidence also, in the records of the period, of reduced wages, and that the hours of work per week in the printing plant had to be curtailed. However, no one was laid off, and the employees of the University of Toronto Press appear to have fared very well during this period in comparison with the hardship that generally prevailed through the printing industry, low though earnings were.

During the first years of World War II, so soon after the Depression, several significant books were issued by the Press, including Douglas Bush: *The Renaissance and English Humanism*; the first volumes of the Mathematical Expositions Series; V. W. Bladen: *An Introduction to Political Economy*; the first edition of W. E. K. Middleton: *Meteorological Instruments*; A. E. Barker: *Milton and the Puritan Dilemma*; and others. These books were well edited, clearly printed, and sturdily bound, although their format does not reveal any awareness on the part of the Press of the typographical revolution which had been taking place in Great Britain in the 1920's and 1930's, or of the standards of book design then being established by some of the leading American university presses. The Press had not added to its stock of type any of the beautiful Monotype fonts then being brought out in the United Kingdom, and for title-pages and chapter-openings could offer only Caslon Old Style (not very attractive in the large sizes), a limited range of Bodoni Bold and Light, and that singularly ugly sans serif face, Kabel. Books were almost invariably set in Monotype Caslon or Binny; as were the journals, except that the *Canadian Journal of Economics and*

Political Science was apt to come out with articles alternating between 10-pt. Binny and 10-pt. Linotype Old Style, depending on the exigencies of the text. Nevertheless, books such as *The Renaissance and English Humanism* and *Milton and the Puritan Dilemma* were so well printed that new editions of them produced in recent years by offset compare creditably with other publications. As the war progressed, however, the quality of paper rapidly declined, and sometimes three or four shades of "white" paper had to be used in one book. Owing to the longevity of university press publications, small quantities of some of these editions still remain on the Press shelves, memorials to the production troubles of that period. Shortage of paper and of labour slowed down book publication; the number of manuscripts accepted for publication in 1944, for example, was only seven, and these took a minimum of two years to publish—one of them, at least, did not emerge until 1947. The journals had a certain advantage in being periodicals—they were frequently off schedule, but at least never failed to appear in proper succession.

In the third year of World War II, Mr. Burns asked for leave of absence to take an active part in the conflict. Leave was granted, and Dr. W. J. Dunlop, Director of University Extension, became Acting Manager. Dr. Dunlop maintained this dual rôle until Mr. Burns returned from service in 1945. (He subsequently became, following his retirement from the University staff, Minister of Education for the Province of Ontario.) In 1942 the Press lost another senior member of its staff. Miss Francess Halpenny, later to become Editor of the Press, who had been appointed to the editorial office on her graduation from the University in 1941, joined the R.C.A.F., Women's Division; she, too, did not return to the Press until 1945.

The year 1945 was significant in the history of the University of Toronto Press. Having served as a member of the Army Personnel Selection Division, and retiring with the confirmed rank of Major, Mr. Burns returned to the managership. He set about at once drafting a report dealing with the immediate needs of the Press. He pointed out the inadequacy of space for all departments—bookstore, publications, and plant; he urged that the appropriation for scholarly publishing should be greatly increased, and that the physical and technical aspects of the production of books be improved. Under the new President of the University, Dr. Sidney E. Smith, the control of the Press was reorganized, and the Press set out on a new policy.

The Committee on Printing and Publications, which since

1929 had dealt with such varied matters as the purchase of a new printing press, the adjustment in salary of a junior employee, the financial problems of the journals, and whether or not to publish scholarly manuscripts, was discontinued. The control of the Press was vested in two bodies, a University Press Committee, which was a sub-committee of the Board of Governors, and an Advisory Committee on Publications, consisting of members of the Faculty. By resolution of the Board of Governors, the function of the new University Press Committee was to be:

1. The elaboration of policy to govern the long and short term objectives of the University Press.
2. The financial control and application of the approved operating policy.
3. The preparation and submission to the Board of Governors from time to time as may be directed or as may be deemed necessary of estimates of the financial requirements for the effective operation of the Press, and the submission to the Board from time to time of a report showing the trend of expenditures in relation to the current estimates.
4. The setting up of a sub-committee to be known as the Publications Committee, comprising selected members of the staff who will serve in an advisory capacity to the management and, if need be, to the Committee itself.

The University Press Committee immediately requested from the Advisory Committee a report recommending a long- and short-term policy for the Publications Department of the Press, and the Committee arranged for three Faculty members, Professors V. W. Bladen, G. W. Brown, and A. S. P. Woodhouse, to visit neighbouring university presses and obtain information about their publishing policies and practices.

Visits were consequently made to Columbia University Press, University of Chicago Press, Harvard University Press, University of Minnesota Press, Princeton University Press, and Yale University Press, and an extensive report, based on these visits and on consideration of the current situation of the Press, was presented to the Advisory Committee, which approved it and passed it on to the Press Committee of the Board of Governors. The six presses visited were prominent members of the Association of American University Presses, which by this time had become an active organization including all the leading university presses in the United States. Its members had developed theories of university press policy and organization and academic publishing philosophies which, while not uniform with all the membership, could be discerned as a general pattern by shrewd observers. The Association's masterly survey, *A Report on*

American University Presses, by Chester Kerr, was still five years in the future, but the three Toronto professors made their own survey and produced a report that in brief anticipated, in many respects, that of Mr. Kerr. The report and the accompanying recommendations of the Committee are too long to be quoted here, or even summarized in full, but *si monumentum quaeris circumspice*. Not every recommendation of the report has been implemented, changing conditions and the Press's own growth have necessitated variations and adaptations, but it turned the Press in 1945 along the path it has been following ever since.

One of the chief recommendations of the report was that the Press should henceforth "have all its profits at its disposal not only for maintenance and replacement, but for necessary expansion and for the support of scholarly publication." Other important recommendations were that an Editor should be appointed (Mrs. Hewitt had retired in 1945 because of family responsibilities), and that the Press "should recognize its obligation to improve the design and workmanship of its production and thereby set a standard for the country." The development of an active publishing policy was strongly advocated, and it was stressed that this policy should include publication of the works of scholars generally, not just of those at the University of Toronto. The report was duly approved by the Board of Governors, and Professor G. W. Brown, formerly Editor of the *Canadian Historical Review*, and a member of the Department of History, was appointed Editor of the Press in June, 1946. His appointment was to be on a part-time basis; in effect, during the next seven years he devoted all the time he could spare from active teaching in the Department of History to the publishing programme of the Press.

The report, in addition to recognizing the need for professional development of the production and design functions of the Press, also spoke of the Press's need of a person qualified to assume the responsibility for organizing and carrying out a continuous and expanding advertising programme. The two jobs were combined in one, and in 1946 the post of Associate Editor and Production Manager was created and assigned to the present writer, a recruit from "commercial" publishing. She had dealt with the problems of editing, production, and advertising in leading Canadian publishing houses, and was, in fact, the first employee to come to the Press with a background of experience in book publishing.

At this time the Press was still hampered by wartime shortages, and a number of books were being manufactured in plants outside the University—some as far away as Regina, Saskatchewan. The quality of a number of these productions left a great deal to be desired, and the problems of remote control permitted little to be done to improve their appearance in proof, beyond some adjustment of title-pages and other final details. The printing staff in the home plant, too, proved at the outset to be strongly resistant to any changes—possibly because during the war years and in the absence of the manager, a great deal of autonomy had developed in the several departments. However, the new Associate Editor arranged to have the contract for the manufacture of a new volume in the Alexander Lectures Series placed with a printer whom she knew well, and this book was designed in detail by her, painstakingly edited by Miss Halpenny, who had returned to the Press and was now senior in the editorial department, and produced with care by the printer. The format of the book, *The Virtues Reconciled*, by Samuel Chew (1947), was approved in most generous fashion by members of the Faculty, and may be said to have turned the tide for good book design at the University of Toronto Press. Within the limits of typefaces and budgets available, nothing but co-operation was encountered in the subsequent improvement of the Press's formats. The Alexander Lectures especially have continued the tradition of decorative design, later volumes having been among the most successful of the many typographic contributions by Antje Lingner of the Publications Production Department.

As an indication of the activity of the Press at this period, we note that in October of 1946, Professor Brown reported that 16 books were currently in the press, 11 were approved for publication in the near future, and 16 manuscripts were in process of consideration. Three years later, in December of 1949, he reported that 21 books had been published in 1946–47, 16 in 1947–48, and 20 in 1948–49. Sixty-four issues of journals had appeared during the same period, and 51 revised editions, reprints, or volumes produced by the Press but not bearing its imprint.

The flow of new manuscripts to the Press for consideration had increased sharply by this time. The programme of grants-in-aid to advanced scholars, begun in 1947 by the Canadian Social Science Research Council (later the Social Science Research Council of Canada) and the Humanities Research Council of Canada, with financial support from the Rockefeller Foundation, began to show its effects. The word that the University Press had increased its programme of subsidizing scholarly publishing was being bruited abroad. The Press had, indeed, increased its subsidizing fund some six times over, but it was still far from adequate. There has been no shortage of publishable scholarly manuscripts from 1945 to the present. The chief embarrassment of the Editor of the Press from 1945 to 1953 was to find enough money and to find enough printing space. However, to maintain perspective, it must be recalled that publication was extremely slow in the scholarly world everywhere in the post-war period, and authors were not subjected to such delays in Canada as they were in Great Britain, for example. The whole situation was indeed a tremendous advance over that of a few years earlier: scholars now could obtain funds for research, and there was at least a reasonable prospect of publication of the products of such effort when completed.

One of the outstanding books published in 1946 was the late R. MacGregor Dawson's *The Government of Canada*, which has remained the standard work in its field since that time. Another notable publication of the period was *The Bella Coola Indians* by T. F. McIlwraith. This 1469-page work in two volumes had been begun in the early war years, put aside during material and labour shortages, resumed in the hope of completing it and releasing the type metal, and again put aside when shortages became even more acute. J. A. Corry's *Democratic Government and Politics*, the first volume to be published in the Canadian Government Series, made its initial bow in 1946. Two new journals were also started. In 1947, the *Canadian Journal of Psychology* was born, and in 1949, the *Canadian Journal of Mathematics*.

The first catalogue the Press had issued since 1935 appeared in the autumn of 1947. It "blurbs" some 43 books, which were titles that had been issued during the past two to three years, or were then in production. The total number of books included is 160. Some of these were survivors of the old "Studies" series, but with pamphlets, out-of-print, and low-stock items eliminated. From that time on, catalogues have been issued by the Press with regularity, and in increasing variety.

During these years the Press was grappling with the task of working out new procedures implementing the new policy with regard to its publications. The function of the Advisory Committee on Publications was by no means clear-cut; the growth of the Press now necessitated a devolution of responsibilities from the top level of administration downwards which was undreamed of in the days of the old Committee on Printing and Publishing. A machinery of reading and reporting on new manuscripts had to be worked out, so that the Advisory Committee could have a satisfactory basis for decision. There was some uncertainty about how the annual sum set aside for the subsidizing of scholarly works should be encumbered by the Press's Accounting Department.

Even in 1947, production in the printing plant was still on an emergency basis. The needs of the University were greatly increased by post-war enrolments. The University had taken over the Government shell-filling plant at Ajax, some thirty miles from Toronto. In addition to establishing a branch bookstore for the needs of the Engineering students who were based at Ajax, the Press took over the operation of a small printing and binding shop which had been part of the Government plant. The student enrolment in the first year at Ajax was 1,800, and in the second, 2,600. In addition to serving the immediate needs of the Engineering courses, the Ajax printing plant was able to take some overflow work from the Press in Toronto. In 1949, the operation was closed and the equipment brought to Toronto.

Despite the assistance of the Ajax presses, new books emerged from the Press at this time with painful slowness. Publications appeared to take second place to every other kind of printing handled by the plant. There was, in fact, urgent need for a scheduling system, although the idea would probably have been laughed to scorn by most of the foremen of that time, who professed to carry—and to a remarkable extent did carry—the details and precise whereabouts of every job in their own heads. The Press's inclusion in the pressmen's strike of 1948, which halted work in most printing houses in the Toronto area, did not assist matters.

The most pressing problem in 1946–49 was, of course, that of physical space. Every autumn, long lines of students waiting to buy their text-books formed along King's College Road and stretched down the side-walk towards College Street. Inside, the space between the entrance and the counter was a mass of struggling humanity. As a "temporary" solution, a one-storey building was erected in 1948 just south of Hart House and east of University College to house the Book Department. This building, however, provided hardly a temporary solution to the *lebensraum* problem of the Press; the congestion in the bookstore at the opening of term was almost as severe as ever, while in the main Press building, the Publications Department overflowed the space allowed for its functions, and each of the manufacturing departments struggled against a stifling congestion of space. Warehousing was inadequately served by a one-storey annex to the Press building, built in 1946.

The need of the Press was undoubtedly departmentalization,

even if this was not fully realized at the time. The introduction of a modern accounting system for the whole Press operation, the development of proper cost accounting for the plant, the maintenance of records of the growing publications inventory, the growth of the editorial office, a more active advertising programme, the increase of Book Department sales—all indicated that the Press was, willy-nilly, sub-dividing into separate operations which required individual organization and supervision.

The Press was still feeling its way among these problems when, in 1949, Mr. Burns, manager of the Press from 1936 to 1942, and from 1945 to 1949, resigned, to be succeeded by Mr. A. G. Rankin. Mr. Rankin, a Chartered Accountant, served as General Manager from 1949 to 1953, and made a particular contribution to the Press by establishing many of the sound accounting procedures which are in use today. In 1951, on his invitation, the Annual Meeting of the Association of American University Presses was held in Toronto. At the conclusion of the sessions, the delegates were entertained by the Press at a memorable banquet in Hart House, where they were addressed by the then Chancellor of the University, His Excellency the Right Honourable Vincent Massey, c.h., recently appointed Governor General of Canada. It was a brilliant occasion, a fitting climax to the University of Toronto Press's fiftieth year of service to the University and the academic world.

Mr. Rankin became Comptroller of the University in the autumn of 1951, but continued part-time as General Manager of the Press until March of 1953; during this period the writer was appointed Assistant General Manager. In March, 1953, Mr. Marsh Jeanneret was appointed executive head of the University of Toronto Press under the new designation of Director. Mr. Jeanneret, a graduate of the University in Honour Law, came to the Press from the Copp Clark Co. Ltd., a long-established firm of educational and general publishers, where he had been Editor of Text-books and a member of the Board of Directors. He had had extensive experience in all phases of book publishing, as well as in printing manufacturing operations, and had travelled widely in Canada. As mentioned earlier, he had, while an undergraduate, worked as a part-time member of the staff of the Press.

The Press had arrived at a crucial stage in its development. As indeed the Chairman of the Board of Governors, Colonel W. E. Phillips, stressed at this time, every business—and the Press was certainly a quasi-business enterprise as well as a department of the University—must constantly move forward or move back;

it cannot stand still. In appointing as Director a young Toronto publisher who was noted for his energy and aggressiveness, the University made plain that its intention was to move forward. In appointing a Director who was by career a publisher, it indicated that its intention was to emphasize and develop the publishing side of the Press's activities.

At the first meeting of the Advisory Committee on Publications following the appointment of the Director, President Smith summarized the purposes of the Press for the benefit of the Committee as follows:

1. To serve the cause of scholarship in the University of Toronto and throughout Canada by supporting a significant scholarly publication programme for books, periodicals, and pamphlets;

2. To publish text-books and other publications from which a profit would be expected;

3. To operate a printing shop which shall provide within the University printing facilities at the lowest possible cost and also provide facilities for profitable operation;

4. To operate a bookstore in the interests of the University community.

In his "preliminary" report to the Advisory Committee, the Director stated that before deciding to come to the Press, he had asked for and received confirmation that the chief purpose of the University of Toronto Press was to support a scholarly publishing programme. He discussed ways and means by which he believed the Press might bring about an expanded programme of publishing scholarly and general works, emphasizing his conviction that the University of Toronto Press must to this end have freedom to develop its general publishing "along sound economic lines, remaining alert to see that our scholarly programme is in no way impaired." Thus the Press would ultimately fulfil in greater measure "the normal functions of leading creative publishers everywhere, including such university presses as Oxford, Cambridge, Columbia, and Chicago."

The growth of the University of Toronto Press since 1953 has proceeded along the lines clearly envisaged by the Board of Governors and by the Director at that time, but at a rate which could hardly then have been anticipated. The number of books published annually, reported as 29 in 1952–53, had increased to 53 in the academic year 1959–60, and in 1960–61 reached the impressive total of 76. In the same eight-year period, the sales of the Printing Department doubled, as did the sales of the Book Department. Sales of the Publications Department quadrupled. The subsidy granted by the Press to scholarly journals in 1953 was practically doubled in 1960, and scholarly books received in 1960 almost three times the amount of financial support from the Press that had been possible in 1953.

Many other notable events in the history of the Press had taken place during these eight years. The Press had constructed a new office and bookstore building at a cost of $500,000, furnished it, and renovated its older building for the exclusive use of the Printing Department, including major capital equipment installations in Composing Room, Pressroom, and Bindery. It had financed all this construction and these purchases out of the proceeds of its own operations. It had also adjusted salary scales so that, for the first time since an editorial office was opened in 1934, editors were paid for their exacting and responsible labours on a scale that compared sensibly with academic salaries. It had climbed to fifth place among university presses in North America in the size of its publishing programme, and it had arrived at a stage when it issued annually more original book-length works than any other Canadian publisher. Its complete list of books in print had risen to 550 volumes. During these eight years, it had published books embodying research of interest to a world-wide audience of scholars. The creative publishing programme had also included the production of many Canadian best-sellers—works that would have honoured the list of any publisher in the world.

The advancement of the publishing programme of the Press was the more remarkable since it was entirely on fronts ordinarily considered peripheral, even foolhardy, in a commercial sense. The Press had no group of British or United States "principals," the sales of whose books would help to carry the overhead. Almost all of its publishing was of a highly cultural, if not academic kind. It issued no school-books; it had no best-selling novelists, no children's authors. Publishing on the financial fringes of the industry, so to speak, the Press could have made errors in judgment, of which the cumulative effect would have been disastrous.

The most important factor in the success of the programme was, of course, the development of sales. The growth of sales, and in particular of publications sales, was no accident. In his report of 1953, Mr. Jeanneret had mentioned his confidence in the editorial, design, and type-composition departments of the Press. Rather significantly, perhaps, he did not refer to its sales promotion of publications, which at this time was handled by one assistant, who used direct mail and display advertising only. The need for direct representation to the trade and libraries was

urgent, particularly if the Press were to discharge its full responsibilities to its authors and to itself. However, at this time the
Press was not publishing enough books that would appeal to
booksellers to justify the employment of even one full-time
representative. A solution was quickly found when in 1954, the
Director of the University of Toronto Press opened negotiations
with the Director of the University of Chicago Press, which
led to the appointment of Toronto as the exclusive selling agent
of Chicago in Canada. However, it was not the intention of the
University of Toronto Press to follow the pattern of a number
of Canadian publishers, and become a sales agent of numerous
foreign presses, rather than a publisher of original works; indeed,
it has, since 1954, declined the requests of many publishers who
have paid it the compliment of suggesting that it become their
representative. But the catalogue of the University of Chicago
Press was in many respects complementary to the Press's, and
it was felt that Chicago and Toronto publications could be
promoted effectively together. Since then the sales in Canada of
both houses have expanded simultaneously, indeed, by a factor
of over four in both cases.

In 1954, the position of Field Representative was created in
order to provide the Press with a much closer editorial and sales
liaison with the trade, libraries, other academic institutions, and
authors across Canada, and to this post was appointed Mr. Hilary
S. Marshall. Mr. Marshall had had experience in law publishing
in both Great Britain and in Canada, and in general publishing
in Canada. With the growth of the Press, Mr. Marshall's
responsibilities have increased; he is now Sales and Advertising
Manager, and his department includes six persons. One of these,
Mr. Desmond Newel, holds the position of Trade and Library
Supervisor. The extensive and diverse activities of Mr. Marshall's
department are described in the chapter which he has contributed
to this book.

Another important step forward in the development of sales
was the appointment in 1954 of sales representatives for the
University of Toronto Press in Continental Europe and in South
America and the Far East. (The Press had been represented in
the United Kingdom by Oxford University Press for a number
of years.) The Director noted in his report of 1954, "The
language barrier obviously provides a lesser handicap to English-
language publishing at the academic level, and the challenge is
chiefly one of promotion and economics." Foreign sales of
scholarly works published by the Press have steadily increased.
Today the Press is still the only Canadian publisher that maintains

a selling organization reaching every part of the world, and it exports more than half its scholarly publications to other countries.

In his report of 1954, made following sixteen months' experience with the three-fold Press operation—publications, printing plant, and bookstore—the Director analyzed the functioning of the Book Department. He pointed out that it was operated on "slightly better than a marginal basis." He stated that the main effort of the Book Department was given to the retailing of short discount educational books, whereas the general bookseller in Canada directed his promotional effort to general books, purchased at a higher discount. The Director drew the conclusion that "inasmuch as the general bookselling trade in Canada is dissatisfied with twice the gross profit margin thus available to our college bookstore, it should be understood that the latter operation cannot be looked to as a subsidizing agent for the publishing programme in the future. That the Bookstore does recover its costs on the narrower margin available on the classification of merchandise it must handle makes it unique in the retail bookselling trade in this country."

The words would have fallen strangely on the ears of R. J. Hamilton. But as retailers in all fields well know, it is not possible to employ competent sales staff at modern wages and enjoy the margin on sales that was possible half a century ago. Even at the time the Students' Book Department was taken over by the Press, the annual statements show no allowance for pensions, for inventory depreciation, for depreciation of building or furniture. At that time the entire staff—including office employees—consisted of four persons, with the addition of student help at busy seasons; today the minimum staff is twenty, and in the rush periods as many as sixty may be employed by the department manager, Mr. Harald Bohne. The University Book Department today absorbs all its own overhead costs; it enjoys no hidden subsidies. To operate the Department on what is, to all intents, a "break-even" basis, requires careful budgeting, close supervision of inventories, and regular study of sales reports. Since the margin between cost and selling-price is so low on most of the stock—20 per cent is the usual discount—the bookstore management cannot afford to make any serious errors in judgment. Miss M. E. MacMurray, Administrative Assistant, draws on many years of experience in her text-book buying, and relies on the co-operation of the Faculty in estimating requirements.

"To operate a bookstore in the interests of the University

community," means more, however, than the distribution of text-books. It means the development of the bookstore as an important cultural centre on the campus, the maintenance of a special-order department that procures individual books from the four corners of the world, the establishment of a periodicals section which may not be expected to show a profit. It means the retention of trained key staff throughout the year, despite low sales during University vacation periods, since the necessary nucleus of trained staff cannot be obtained on a temporary basis. It means, in the University of Toronto with its varied courses, the carrying of an inventory of some fifteen thousand individual titles. The bookstore of the University of Toronto, which sells books, a wide range of international cultural periodicals, and stationery, does not resemble in the least the typical "College Store" of the United States, with its cameras, sports equipment, transistor radios, lingerie, and soda fountain.

To operate the University bookstore in the interests of the University community in this broad sense, however, required not only the will to extend its service, but the physical space in which to do it. In 1954, accommodation was inadequate for such development. In a special report to the President and the Press Committee of the Board of Governors on October 25, 1954, the Director of the Press recommended:

> Erection of a new Press building to comprise all the following departments . . . (a) Bookstore, (b) Publications Department . . . (c) Accounting Department . . . (d) Administrative departments. The purpose of the above building would be to provide an academic centre on the campus for all Press activities except the processing of actual printing orders, and to establish the publishing activities of the press in a situation that would encourage their maximum use by the University community. . . . A site might be the area east of the new University Extension Building, facing south-east toward the front campus. . . . The Press appears to possess the financial ability to underwrite all normal building and alterations costs . . . without additional grants from other University funds.

Within three years, on the strength of the advance made by the Press up to that time, authority to proceed with a new building had been granted by the Board of Governors. It was opened officially by President Claude T. Bissell on December 6, 1958.

The physical limitations suffered by the Book Department in its temporary building south of the old Observatory had been accompanied by more than a few psychological handicaps, since the building was highly unpopular from the outset as an architectural feature. With the Gothic glories of Hart House looming above it, and the Romanesque charm of University College on the west, it was generally regarded as a wen on the campus.

In the main Press building, the space formerly occupied by the Book Department had been absorbed without any easing of the pressure. Steps were taken to make optimum use of the limited space available. The editorial office had been housed in Baldwin House with the Department of History since 1934, although several of its members were by now located in the main building. In 1953, however, the entire staff was brought into the Press building, and the Accounting Department removed to Baldwin House, the balance of which was then occupied by the Faculty of Law, during one stage of the latter's pilgrimages.

This change brought both the office of the Director and the publications production staff into advantageous proximity to the editorial staff, while the business machines which had competed with the rumbling of the presses and the crash of the guillotine in the bindery were able to chatter away more cheerfully to themselves in the seclusion of Baldwin House. However, conditions were still far from ideal, especially when the number of authors conferring with editors increased, to the disturbance of those who were trying to concentrate on manuscripts; the business departments of both Publications and Printing also became more active. The departure of the Faculty of Law to Glendon Hall in 1957 opened the way for the Press to take over the whole of Baldwin House, and the Editorial, Production, Accounting, and Administrative staffs settled with great relief into the new quarters, leaving the whole of the original Press building for the use of the manufacturing department.

Minor structural alterations were made in Baldwin House to accommodate the Press personnel, and although the building was not ideally suited to its new purposes, it was a veritable haven after the earlier congestion. The chief drawback was the number and size of the rooms; the building contained a small number of large offices, rather than a larger number of small offices. The removal of the Administrative offices from the Printing Department building and their distribution over a large building, however, led to the establishment of media of communication—routines of mail-handling, telephone connections, "intercom" equipment, and messenger service—which were a useful preparation for the greater physical separation which was to take place a year and a half later.

The Printing Department now occupies the whole of the original Press building built in 1920, and extended in 1926 and 1946. By 1961 the staff of this department alone had grown to one hundred—just double that of 1945. Equipment has been modernized and the space has been fully utilized but not expanded, following the policy laid down in 1953. The Director of the University of Toronto Press has steadily emphasized that the Printing Department was not, and should not become, a competitor of commercial printers in the Toronto area. He has frequently directed the attention of the craftsmen themselves, as well as of the trades unions to which they belong and the printing trade generally, to the fact that a very large part of the printing done by the University of Toronto Press is of a kind that would not occur if this institution did not exist to foster it. The successful operation of the Press provides the margin with which to subsidize the scholarly works that would otherwise never be put into print, and never provide work for the industry, either within or outside the University. The efficient operation of the Printing Department thus, in effect, actually *creates* work.

The complex nature of the Printing Department operation was pointed up by a survey of the previous year's printing orders made in 1955. Although the volume of book and other manufacturing orders averaged many thousands of dollars each, the survey indicated that the median value of all the manufacturing orders executed by the Press was exactly seventeen dollars. It was clear that the services of the manufacturing department could not be as selective as those of a purely commercial printing establishment: the Press could not choose the types of work it preferred or refuse kinds that were not remunerative; it had to administer a wide range of services as efficiently as possible.

Mr. Roy Gurney became Plant Superintendent in 1950, having first served as Estimator. He had had a thorough training in the well-known and long-established printing house of Rous & Mann, which has bred many executives for the printing industry in Toronto; he had also experienced for a period the problems of owner-managership. Under Mr. Gurney, the programme of modernization and expansion of manufacturing facilities began in 1953, and has continued to the present. The Assistant Superintendent, Mr. F. Strutt, was appointed to this new post in 1960; he had already brought to the Press a wide supervisory experience in the printing trade. Mrs. Anne E. Hill, who had previously served as Publications Supervisor, became Administrative Assistant in the Printing Department in 1957.

The modernization of the printing plant has been carried forward entirely at the Press's expense, with the approval and under the review of the Board of Governors. The constant objective has been the establishment of a printing plant which would be one of the most modern of its kind in Canada, able to provide the versatile services required by the University. The result has been to increase the capacity of the plant and achieve manufacturing economies, without enlargement of the plant building. Nevertheless, it is intended that in the future the Press will sub-contract an increasing proportion of routine printing and binding work to outside suppliers. Thus the University Press should become a more and more valuable customer of the local printing trade, and at the same time maintain its own highly specialized plant, with an ever more excellent ratio of chargeable to non-chargeable time. The desirability of such a condition will be apparent to everyone acquainted with the costing of manufacturing operations.

Before the decision was made to construct a new Press building on the campus for the other departments, serious consideration was given to the advisability of re-locating the printing plant off the campus. Within the past decade, many printing houses have moved from downtown Toronto to the suburbs. Initially, the possibility of constructing a modern plant building at low cost in a suburban location seemed very attractive. However, after the survey made in 1955, which exposed the large proportion of small orders handled by the Press, each requiring much administrative handling in relation to its dollar value, it was concluded that if the plant were re-located off the campus it would have to restrict rather than expand its former kind of service to the University community.

The renovation of the printing plant has included the renewal and replacement of outmoded equipment, the addition of new equipment designed to reduce expensive hand labour and to improve the quality of production, and the introduction of new procedures leading to greater efficiency both in the office and in the shop. The records of the University Press over the years show that, save in times of stress such as the world wars or the Great Depression, additions were steadily made to the equipment of the plant. They tended, however, to be made in fits and starts. At no time previously was there established a regular programme of research and renewal such as has been adhered to during the most recent decade.

The introduction of a modern scheduling system into the printing plant, beginning in 1954, has been effective not only in improving the efficiency of the plant, but in improving relations with its customers. The public relations of an institution-owned enterprise such as the University printing plant are necessarily a delicate responsibility. Such monopoly as it enjoys of University printing is in fact a monopoly of convenience only, and its good relations with individual members of the University staff who deal with it must be very carefully maintained. These customers must be served to the best of the Press's ability, and over the years the Press has had many employees whose loyalty to the University has been outstanding. In turn, customers of the Press have become increasingly aware that good service is being given. The scheduling system has been a valuable factor here. By this means each customer is informed in advance when his work will reach each stage of production, and if the scheduling does not fit into his own plans and requirements, plant and customer have the opportunity to work out a better plan together. Proper scheduling eliminates many emergencies; when one does arise, the co-operation of the craftsmen of the University Press is marvellous. The writer remembers one occasion when the scheduled date for delivery of a convention programme had been overlooked by the customer; she was informed of this at 6 p.m. on a Friday afternoon of a summer week-end. Within an hour of the time she communicated with the Foreman of the Composing Room, the latter had rounded up every member of his staff still in the city; the plant hummed on Saturday and Sunday, and on Monday morning the programmes were at the convention hall at 8:45 a.m., as required.

By 1957, the growth of the plant, and the improvement in production, had arrived at the point where the need for its own design and typographic service was felt. Mr. Harold Kurschenska, a young compositor-typographer, was engaged. The development of his talent has been watched with sympathetic interest by both the printing plant and the Publications Department, which also frequently uses his services. His designs are fresh and modern, and his range of invention seems inexhaustible. This book is one of his formats.

Good design, however, is virtually ineffectual if it is not backed up by good production. Throughout the printing plant, there is today an interest in good typography, in fine presswork, and in quality binding, which is stimulating to the further efforts of typographers and designers. The proofreading service has developed in its own dramatic way, as a part of a general system of quality control maintained through the plant, in which the entire staff, supervisors and craftsmen alike, participate fully.

The acquisition of new Linotype and Monotype fonts, long overdue, together with foundry and display type, and various fonts for the Ludlow Typesetting machine purchased in 1956, culminated in the publication in 1958 of *Type Faces*, a substantial catalogue of the many fonts and special characters available at the Press. Each copy was numbered and supplied to a designated recipient, and as new pages, with new fonts and sizes, are added, the books are brought up to date. For its examples of typesetting of text, the Press used, instead of sentences such as the "quick brown fox jumps over the lazy dog," Milton's noble paragraph which begins, "He who destroys a good Book, kills reason itself, kills the Image of God, as it were in the eye. Many a man lives a burden to the Earth; but a good Book is the precious life-blood of a master-spirit, embalmed and treasured up on purpose to a life beyond life. . . ."

In 1956, the University of Toronto Press began to use its own printer's mark to distinguish its publications. This design was derived from the official crest of the University, and thus reflects the Press's relationship to its parent institution, although it does not reproduce the official crest as such—for the Press acts as publisher for the whole Canadian academic world, not for just its own campus. This printer's emblem, which includes the tree, the crown, the books, and the beaver, well reflects the activities and associations of the University of Toronto Press. It appears on a majority of Press publications, on letterheads, labels, posters, and other ephemera, and is even used as a water-mark on University Bond, a paper stock manufactured to Press specifications. However, when the Press is acting as printer for the University, as distinct from publisher, the official crest of the University is employed.

The ability of the printing plant to produce good books received a major stimulation when the entire original Press building was turned over to it in 1957. In 1958, a new Press building provided equivalent stimulation to the University Book Department and the Publications Department. The building predicted by the Director in 1954 had become a reality, and on the precise spot first recommended. As he had also foretold, the Press was able to finance the building itself. In eighteen months, the building was planned in detail, constructed, and occupied. In a single day during July of 1958, the Editorial, Publications, Accounting, and Administrative departments moved from Baldwin House to the second and third floors of the new three-storey building on the north-west of the campus, and a few weeks later the Book Department left its "temporary" structure, in which it had operated for ten years, and established itself on the main floor of the new building.

The ground floor of the new Press Building is designed to permit the Book Department complete flexibility in arrangement of fixtures. The illuminated showcases can be arranged to provide adequate counter area for the text-book rush in the autumn, when all the display stands and racks are moved out of the way of the crowds of students. Then, when the rush is over, the fixtures and showcases are regrouped to provide attractive browsing displays throughout the rest of the year. The second floor was designed to include open office areas for accounting and order handling, and private offices for administrative heads. On the third floor, individual private offices of modest size for the editorial and designing staff were provided. A central lunch room on the second floor provides facilities for staff members lunching in, and a reference library on the third floor is used for regular staff meetings. The basement of the building was planned for use partly as an additional selling area, and partly for warehousing current stock. Until recently, it held publications inventory, and wholesale shipping operations were also conducted from it. It had not been anticipated, however, that on the crowded University of Toronto campus it would be economical to provide storage space permanently, and outside storage has been rented for some years. In 1961, the Press leased 10,000 square feet of space in a new building downtown, where both publications book stock and plant paper stock are warehoused; shipping of publications is now also carried on from this warehouse. Mr. J. McDonough and Mr. F. Malcher are in charge of the new warehouse.

While the ashlar stone exterior of the new Press Building is traditional in style, to blend with the architecture of neighbouring University buildings, the interior is modern. Walls are in cheerful colours, and advantage is taken of corridor space for the mounting of photographic portraits of all Press authors, now totalling well over two hundred. Special emphasis was laid upon adequate lighting, and those engaged in the most detailed editorial, proofreading, and accounting functions have found the illumination excellent. The total number of staff members accommodated in the new Press Building averaged one hundred in 1961.

The office operations of the Publications Department were combined in 1958 with similar operations of the Bookstore, and both placed under the direction of Mr. Harald Bohne, Manager of the Bookstore. Mr. Bohne had come to the Press with experience in library work in Germany, and in publishing in Canada. Mrs. Eileen Jones was appointed Administrative Assistant in the Book Department office in 1960.

The Accounting Department, on the second floor of the new

Press Building, is directed by Mr. J. G. Garden, Chief Accountant, who was appointed to this post in 1954, following the departure of Mr. D. J. Reid, when the latter became Chief Accountant of the University. Mr. Garden brought to the Press many years' experience in book publishing, which he was able to apply to the particular problems of the Press—one of his first steps, for example, was to introduce a simple invoice-copy system to handle the multitudinous single-order accounts-receivable of the Press. His department, in the administration of which he has been assisted by Mr. S. Redhill, Accountant, since 1955, and by Mr. K. Williams, Accounting Assistant, since 1959, provides, in addition to the ordinary accounting of any business house, the specialized cost accounting and reports required by the printing plant and management. The monthly, quarterly, and annual statements issued by the Accounting Department furnish the office of the Director, and the Board of Governors of the University, a detailed picture of the Press's operations at all times. The comprehensive nature of these reports is made apparent by even such a partial listing as the following:

1. Annual Statement, including:
   Balance Sheet
   Income and Expense Statement
   Operating Statements of each Department (8 in all).
2. Annual Budget, in same form as above.
3. Monthly Operating Statements, in same form as above, but including year to date, previous year to date, month in question, previous year's total operations, current year's approved budget, proportion of budget for year to date, and estimated actual for current year.
4. Subsidiary reports, giving details on which the various statements are based, such as publications sales reports by title and by category.
5. Printing Department reports:
   a. Daily report by cost centre analyzing chargeable and non-chargeable time and output
   b. Weekly report showing deviations from normal cost recovery by individual dockets
   c. Monthly report by cost centre, giving comparison with budget of hours worked, chargeable and non-chargeable time, and cost recovery.
6. Daily report of sales by departments for Book Department.

The number and nature of these accounting reports attest to the complexity of the University of Toronto Press organization today. They are also evidence of the method used in carrying out the policy of recent years, which has been to convert the Press from an administrative liability, as it seems to have been at times regarded, to an organization which reports to the University administration and secures the latter's approval of its actions, but tries not to distract the administration with problems it should try to digest itself—always keeping in mind that its authority is derived from the Board of Governors of the University, and that it is responsible to the Board.

By achieving economic success, and maintaining an effective organization, the Press has undoubtedly won a greater measure of confidence from both the University administration and the academic staff, and this confidence has strengthened it for further achievements.

In the new Press Building, the publishing departments have been able to expand to their full potential, and the rapid increase in numbers of publications and in sales reflects the benefits of improved working conditions. The enlarged Editorial Department, consisting in 1961 of twenty persons, is headed by Miss Halpenny, who was appointed Editor of the Press in 1957. Her Associate Editors are Miss Jean Houston and Miss Jean Jamieson, who have played a large part in building up the valuable relationships with authors which have been such a strong feature of the department. Miss Barbara Plewman became Publications Production Manager in 1957 also. From 1959 to 1961 the list of publications jumped from 40 to 72, while sales of publications increased 75 per cent. As Canada became more and more frequently host to large international congresses, the Editorial and Publications Production departments took on the responsibility of seeing Congress Proceedings, and frequently Programmes and Abstracts, through the press, while the Publications Department supervised their distribution and general sale. Some of these Proceedings have been of great size, such as *Geology of the Arctic*, published in 1961 (over twelve hundred pages, with illustrations, and accompanying maps and charts), and *Recent Advances in Botany*, which appeared in the autumn of the same year and totalled eighteen hundred pages. The number of journals sponsored and subsidized by the Press increased to ten by 1961, and all of these but two were quarterlies. That the Editorial Department was able to absorb this great volume of work without apparent strain testified to the strength of the organization which had been built up.

In 1959 the Editorial Department began work on a vast project which had been in prospect for some years. A prominent businessman of Toronto, Mr. James Nicholson, who died in 1952, bequeathed to the University a large portion of his estate, for the specific purpose of founding a Dictionary of Canadian

Biography. While the idea of such a Dictionary had been under consideration at the Press for many years, the financial problem had hitherto seemed insurmountable. In the words of Dr. George Brown, this inheritance was for the academic world "manna from Heaven." However, under the will, the University had been made a residuary legatee only, and it was not until 1959 that arrangements were made, largely through the efforts of Mr. F. Stone, Vice-President of the University, for the bulk of the legacy to be released so that work on the Dictionary might begin. By this time the estate had accumulated in value so that rather more than a million dollars was available—but, it must be added, on an endowment basis, which meant that only the income could be used; thus current work on the Dictionary had to be carefully budgeted. On the recommendation of the Director of the Press, the President of the University appointed, in April, 1959, Dr. George Brown, Honorary Editor of the Press since 1954, as first General Editor of the Dictionary of Canadian Biography. The public received the announcement of the foundation of the Dictionary with enthusiasm. In June, 1960, Miss Elizabeth Loosley was appointed Assistant to the General Editor.

The Nicholson bequest is the largest single contribution which the Press has received in aid of subsidized publication, and one of the largest such gifts ever made for publishing purposes. During the past decade, however, the Press has also received substantial support from many organizations and agencies. The Social Science Research Council of Canada and the Humanities Research Council, both before and after the establishment of the Canada Council, have been generous in their grants to scholarly publications as has the Canada Council itself. Almost invariably, of course, the Publications Fund of the Press (as the annual amount set aside by the Press with the approval of the Board of Governors for the subsidization of scholarly works is called) has borne the major portion of the expense of publication, but the Fund has been able to stretch much farther to cover a greater body of publishing, by reason of such assistance. In 1957 the Press received the first of a series of annual grants from the Ford Foundation for publication in the humanities and social sciences; by 1961, the total received from this source had amounted to $42,500. This grant developed from, but was not an integral part of, the simultaneous programme carried on by the Ford Foundation with university presses in the United States. The University of Toronto Press has also collaborated frequently with Canadian universities without presses of their own in publication of subsidized or partly subsidized works, providing editorial, production and distribution services to these other institutions.

The growth of the general publishing programme of the Press (that is, of books expected to have a general appeal to the public) has been remarkable. In the last decade the Press has published a number of "best-sellers" which sometimes have been, and sometimes have not been, classifiable as "academic" titles as well. But it is notable that in each instance a special contribution has been made, either in editing or in production, which the University of Toronto Press was almost uniquely qualified to provide. Indeed, some such books have come to the Press largely because of the desire of the author to make use of the Press's special services. As long ago as 1950, Dr. Sherwood Fox brought to Toronto his intriguing regional study, *The Bruce Beckons*. He proposed that the Press should publish this book, and after some hesitation (induced partially by an adverse reader's report, which contradicted the views of the Press's own editorial department), the Press agreed to do so. The book, published in 1953, was an immediate best-seller, the first in the experience of many members of the Press staff.

Towards the end of 1953, the Press became interested in a manuscript then in process of completion, dealing with the sociology of a North American suburb—which happened to be in the Toronto area. The possibilities of the manuscript were so apparent that the Director committed the Press, in principle, to publish *Crestwood Heights* after reading the first fifteen pages. The book, by John Seeley, R. Alexander Sim, and Elizabeth W. Loosley, was published in 1956, and, not in the least to the Press's surprise, became a best-seller. Indeed, *Crestwood Heights* caused a flurry in advance of its appearance. Simultaneous publication had been arranged with a United States publisher for a specified date, and care was taken not to release even advance copies too early, because of the controversial nature of the material. But an enterprising reporter "borrowed" an advance copy of the United States edition from a book display at a convention of psychologists in Chicago, and summarized the contents for his newspaper in Toronto. The source of his scoop remained a mystery for several days, while the Press was bombarded by indignant representatives of the other Toronto papers. In the end, over 55 linear feet of Canadian newspaper columns were devoted to the book.

At the same time, another best-seller was in the making. While Mackenzie King was still living, the Press had written to express interest in publishing his memoirs, and he had replied pleasantly, but, characteristically, without leaving the Press perfectly clear as to his intentions. But when Dr. R. MacGregor Dawson was appointed in 1950 to prepare the official biography from the late Prime Minister's papers, our interest deepened, if possible, for although Mr. King's feelings towards his alma mater might or might not be kindly (in view of certain famous events of his undergraduate career), the Press had long enjoyed close associations with Dr. Dawson, who was the author of the classic text, *The Government of Canada*, and General Editor of the Government of Canada Series. However, the University of Toronto Press was by no means the only Canadian publisher interested in securing the right to publish the late Prime Minister's biography, and Dr. Dawson was, quite naturally, aware that he had a literary property of considerable value at his disposal. The Director and the Assistant Director of the Press remember vividly a long sunny afternoon in the Park Plaza Hotel in Toronto during which they finally came to an agreement with Dr. Dawson to publish the work. One of their chief inducements was the promise that the manuscript would be edited personally by Miss Halpenny, who had put Dr. Dawson's previous books through the press. (A favourite anecdote of Dr. George Brown describes how Dawson called to him down the hall of Baldwin House one day from an editorial conference in Miss Halpenny's office—and nobody ever had any trouble in hearing Dawson— "George, this young lady's got me down, and now she's going over me with a harrow.") The Director and Assistant Director came away from that afternoon's interview with Dr. Dawson not only with Volume I of the biography, but an interesting recommendation to revive the *Canadian Annual Review*—a suggestion which came to fruition in 1961.

As it happened, the Press's editorial contribution to the King biography was large, and it is no disrespect to Dr. Dawson's memory to say so, for death interrupted this brilliant scholar and careful craftsman. The index for the volume was compiled by Miss Halpenny while on vacation in Muskoka. To the amusement, but not surprise of her colleagues, she was so absorbed in her task that a large motor-launch burned and sank, its occupants being rescued from the water, some fifty yards from the cottage where she was working without her being aware of it.

The editorial and administrative offices of the Press were still in Baldwin House when the Director first discussed with Mr. Floyd Chalmers of Maclean-Hunter, over a luncheon table, the idea of publishing a de luxe volume of portraits by Yousuf

Karsh, and when the first specifications for the elaborate production were discussed with Mr. Paul Arthur, and when the first request for estimate on sheet-fed gravure was sent to Enschedé in Haarlem—a house recommended to the Director by contacts he had made in Holland when on a business trip the previous year. But the Press had erected its new building and lived in it for a year, before the production of *Portraits of Greatness* had been completed to the exacting specifications of the artist-author, the designer, and the Press, and the book launched on its epoch-making career. Thirty-eight thousand copies have now been printed in English and an edition in German is in preparation.

The academic year 1960–61 produced several important publishing events. The Hon. J. W. Pickersgill's *The Mackenzie King Record*, Vol. I, *1939–44*, published in the autumn of 1960, won both scholarly applause and a wide general sale. In March of 1961, the University of Toronto Press and Les Presses de l'Université Laval made the joint announcement that the Dictionary of Canadian Biography would be published simultaneously in French and English, the French edition, entitled *Dictionnaire Biographique du Canada*, to be sponsored and published by Laval. This is beyond all doubt the most outstanding example of bicultural co-operation in Canada that has occurred to date, and it comes as a climax to a continuous programme of bilingual publication carried out by the University of Toronto Press. This programme has ranged from the publication of journals in which French articles are regularly interspersed with those written in English; to bilingual books with authors contributing in their native language, whether French or English; to bibliographies of works in both languages; to special studies of French-English relations in Canada. It is accurate to say that at the University of Toronto Press, among compositors and proofreaders and editors, French is truly regarded as one of our two national languages.

In the spring of 1961, the University of Toronto Press published the *Canadian Annual Review for 1960*, edited by John T. Saywell. Publication of this volume, much needed by librarians and scholars, who had long urged the beginning of such a work, was assisted by a generous grant from the Canada Council, and by financial support from the Press itself. The large task of securing able contributions, editing the entire work, and writing an important article himself, was performed by Professor Saywell on a tight schedule.

The University of Toronto Press has always endeavoured to be a good citizen: it has participated fully in joint activities in the printing industry, in the bookselling trade, and in publishing. Sometimes it has done this when its own interests were remote indeed, as in the case of "Young Canada's Book Week." The Press was a member of the original Toronto Typothetae, as mentioned in the early pages of this history, and later joined the Toronto Graphic Arts Council, subsequently known as the Toronto Graphic Arts Association. In 1946–47 and 1947–48, Mr. A. Gordon Burns, Manager of the Press, was President of this Association. In 1949, Mr. Burns was Vice-President of the Canadian Graphic Arts Association. For fifteen years, he was the representative of the Toronto Board of Trade on the Advisory Vocational Committee of the Toronto Board of Education. In addition to being a member of the Graphic Arts Industries Association, the Press is a member of the Council of Printing Industries, and the Book Manufacturers' Institute.

The Printing Department staff actively supports the International Association of Printing House Craftsmen; nine staff members belong to the Association at the present time. The Plant Superintendent, Mr. R. Gurney, was President of the Toronto Club in 1958–59, an International Governor in 1959–61, Vice-President of the International Association in 1961–62, and is President-Elect for 1962–63. He is the first Canadian to become a Governor of this world-wide association, which has more than 120 member clubs on five continents.

All manufacturing departments of the University Press are operated under union contracts, and the policy of the Press has been to support union contractual obligations in every way possible. Since the Press is not conducted for the purpose of making a financial profit for the University, but with the object of creating a surplus which may be expended on subsidized publishing, thus creating more work for the craftsmen of the Press, the interests of management and staff in maintaining the financial health of the Press are identical; they are not in competition for profits, since all net income is expended on more publishing.

The University of Toronto Press has been an active member of the Canadian Booksellers' Association since the inception of the latter. Mr. Harald Bohne, Manager of the University Book Department, was Chairman of the College Section in 1960–62, and Vice-President of the Association for 1961–62. Miss Margaret MacMurray, Administrative Assistant, was appointed Convention Chairman for 1959 and for 1962. The Press is also a member of the National Association of College Stores, and the American Booksellers Association (Associate Member).

As a publisher, the University of Toronto Press is an active member of the Canadian Book Publishers Council, and of the Book Publishers' Association of Canada. The Director of the Press is Chairman of the Standing Committee on Copyright in the former body. The Press has long been a member of the Association of American University Presses, and members of its staff have served on its executive and on various committees. An invitation has been extended to the Association to hold its Annual Meeting again in Toronto in 1967, during the celebration of the Confederation centenary. As previously mentioned, the Press is the only Canadian member of this Association, but ranks among the first half-dozen in size.

The generous support given to the Press's publications programme by librarians is acknowledged by the Press's Contributing Membership in the Canadian Library Association. Individual members of the Press editorial staff belong to professional organizations such as the Humanities Association of Canada, the Canadian Historical Association, the Canadian Political Science Association, and many others. The Press has for long been publisher to the Royal Society of Canada, of which Dr. George W. Brown is Honorary Editor, and has participated in the modern publishing programme of the Society, which has brought the fruits of research reported by its Fellows to a much wider public through books for general distribution. Various members of the Editorial Department regularly attend the learned societies' annual meetings, and recent publications of the Press are exhibited for the interest of the societies—many of whose members are, of course, authors of books published by the Press.

The story of the University of Toronto Press would not be complete without a tribute to the loyalty of its staff. The Press has been fortunate in having throughout the years a large number of employees with a record of long and faithful service. For example, Miss Eva Walker, who retired in 1957, had been with the Press for 42 years. Miss Walker, Secretary of the Press; Mr. J. Weir, Foreman of the Composing Room from 1929 to 1952; Mr. John Conway, journeyman compositor from 1922 to 1957; Mr. John Manuel, bookbinder, from 1927 to 1952; Mr. Leo Grant, pressman (1920–   ), Mr. Arthur Verrall (1917–   ), Stockroom Supervisor; Mr. Howard Albin (1924–   ), Foreman of the Bindery; Miss Grace Verrall (1925–   ), bindery; Mr. James Taylor (1929–   ), Production Planner; and Mr. E. Ottaway (1931–   ), bindery, were all with the Printing Department through the trying years of the Great Depression and World War

II. The records of the Press reveal many other instances of extended service during the existence of this institution. The present Foreman of the Composing Room, Mr. Kenneth Allen, and the Foreman of the Pressroom, Mr. C. Wyatt, served for several years on the staff before being appointed to their present positions.

In the spring of 1959, a monthly house organ, entitled *Press Notes*, was founded under the editorship of the Assistant Director. At first its distribution was to members of the Press staff only, but following many indications of wider interest, it was circulated to the University of Toronto staff generally, and to a number of other friends of the Press in academic institutions across Canada. *Press Notes* publishes articles giving factual information on different phases of university press publishing, on special projects of the Press, on book production and printing problems, and gives news of staff members, Press authors, and new publications. *Press Notes* has appeared regularly every month since its establishment. A notable feature has been the number of technical articles contributed by the craftsmen of the Printing Department.

As the University of Toronto Press approached its sixtieth year, a new Canadian university press was born—McGill University Press, founded July 1, 1960. This was the first proof in all that time that the university press tradition was taking hold in Canada, and the event was welcomed enthusiastically. The University of Toronto Press looks forward to a long and friendly rivalry with this new press, which it hopes may soon be joined by presses at several other Canadian universities. Already an arrangement has been made with McGill University Press for the selling of McGill books in Toronto by University of Toronto Press, and of Toronto books in Montreal by McGill University Press. The scope for reciprocal assistance among several Canadian university presses yet unborn is great indeed.

In comparison with some university presses of the Old World, the history of the University of Toronto Press covers a short span of years. In comparison with the greater number of university presses of the New World, the Press is already venerable. Its future is unknown to us; but as an integral part of the University, it may well continue as long as this great University itself. To have played a part in the development of an institution destined in all probability for so long a life is an honour keenly appreciated by all who have made their contribution to it in this generation. To have played our part in this era when Canadian scholarship and culture were coming to flower has been a special privilege. It is good to know that the contribution made by the Press in our day will remain as long as the books stand on the library shelves of the world.

The words we write now may seem quaint to those who inherit our responsibilities at the University of Toronto Press. If the world changes as rapidly in the next sixty years as it has from 1901 to 1961, this will certainly be true. But to our successors we would say, even if the words seem quaint: in our time we have tried, we wish you well in yours.

The Scholarly Books of the University of Toronto Press

Francess Halpenny

The general purpose of the subsidized programme of publication of the University of Toronto Press, as indeed of any university press, is to make available the results of scholarly research which might not otherwise be adequately published. In this statement lies the chief reason for the creation of any university press and an implication of its necessarily intimate association with the academic world. It is, of course, true that a university press will accept for its list works of scholarship, appropriate non-fiction, even creative literature, which do not require subsidy. These, too, however, will almost always reflect the academic association, and their assistance in the form of net returns from sales is of special value because it can be put at the service of manuscripts worthy of publication but not strong enough commercially to achieve it unaided.

The administration of a subsidized programme of scholarly publications will differ among various presses, and the differences will often reflect the manner in which a press has been organized initially and how it relates to its parent institution. Thus this book describes how the programme is carried out at the University of Toronto Press, but its procedures actually reflect general patterns followed at most university presses, with, of course, some variations peculiar to Toronto.

The need for a formal description of the book publication programme of the University of Toronto Press had been recognized for some time when, in 1960, a report was prepared on current policy and procedures, and presented to the Advisory Committee on Publications. The Committee, accordingly, adopted the report as a statement of policy, and this article is based closely on that statement.

Subsidies for scholarly book publication are provided from

the Publications Fund of the University of Toronto Press. This Fund is maintained by annual grants authorized by the Board of Governors of the University, on the recommendation of the Director, entirely from the proceeds of the Press's operations, and without assistance—either direct or indirect—from other University funds. At the present time, out of total grants of over eighty thousand dollars, the sum of approximately fifty thousand dollars is devoted annually to the support of publication of scholarly books. The balance is devoted to the support of the scholarly journals bearing the Press's imprint. In practice, the total costs of production of subsidized books approved for publication are charged to the Fund at the time they are incurred, and net proceeds from the sales of these books are credited to the Fund as they accrue. In this way the Fund accumulates revenue beyond the subsidies voted annually, and makes possible a correspondingly larger amount of publishing.

The Publications Fund is administered by the Advisory Committee on Publications, which is composed of senior members of the University staff representing the major disciplines, with the President as Chairman and the Director of the Press as Secretary. Scholarly manuscripts are given first consideration by the Editorial Department of the University Press; if not declined at this stage they may then be submitted to carefully selected readers for expert opinions in the particular field of study to which each belongs. Appropriate fees are paid to the readers and the identity of those reporting is held in strict confidence, normally being shared only with the Advisory Committee. Manuscripts recommended by readers' reports are brought forward for consideration by the Committee at its next regular meeting. Ordinarily, the Committee does not examine the actual manuscripts, but meets to appraise the reports received and make a decision based on this appraisal.

The Advisory Committee's ability to approve for publication is of course limited by budgetary considerations at any time. It also recognizes some natural priorities of interest in addition to the first priority of merit. Manuscripts written by Canadian scholars, or on subjects relating to Canada, or presenting results of research carried out in Canada, are generally felt to have some priority of claim on the Fund, all other considerations being equal. Reprints of scholarly works previously published elsewhere, or translations of published works, necessarily have a low priority. No special priority has been granted works written at this University, and rather more than half the works subsidized by the Press represent scholarship at other institutions.

The financial support given to manuscripts through the Publications Fund is frequently augmented by smaller additional subsidies previously offered to their authors by councils such as the Social Science Research Council of Canada, the Humanities Research Council, and, of recent years, the Canada Council, or by other universities and institutions. (Personal subsidies by authors of manuscripts are accepted only under very exceptional circumstances.) Grants made by the Councils are also usually based on reports from qualified readers. Although a grant of assistance towards publication by a Council does not mean automatic acceptance by the Advisory Committee of the Press, the recommendations of its readers will carry great weight. An important difference between the activities of the Councils and the Advisory Committee is that the Councils may give support to research as such, whereas the Publications Fund is used to support only the results of research as embodied in actual manuscripts.

A collateral grant of great importance to scholars publishing in the humanities and social sciences has been received in recent years from the Ford Foundation. This grant, which is subject to numerous conditions that parallel the Press's own conditions with regard to subsidizing book publication, has amounted to $8,500 per year over a five-year period beginning in 1957, annual renewal being based on audited reports supplied by the Press to the Ford Foundation each year.

Manuscripts subsidized by the Publications Fund are published under the same contractual arrangements with regard to royalties as are non-subsidized books; they are produced as attractively and promoted as vigorously, each in its proper market. Each manuscript will be edited to a standard carefully set and maintained by the Editorial Department of the Press. All details of format, including the selection of type, layout of pages, choice and arrangement of illustrations, the kind of paper, binding and jacket, will be planned by the Publications Production Department with a view to displaying the content suitably and to the best advantage. Scholarship is not purer scholarship because it comes forth in drab apparel; an attractive but dignified format will do much to attract readers to it. The Promotion Department will prepare descriptive literature, send out review copies, and plan sales campaigns including exhibits, newspaper advertisements, extensive direct mail circularization, and personal calls on booksellers and scholars: its objective is optimum distribution within the community to which the work is addressed.

The list of scholarly publications made possible by the operation of such a publications fund is a source of pride with any university press. Here at Toronto it has enabled the founding of a number of scholarly series, individual entries in which frequently receive collateral assistance from one of the research councils. These series include the University of Toronto Romance Series (founded 1948), the Department of English Studies and Texts (founded 1942), and the University of Toronto Near and Middle East Series (founded 1948). In 1946, the Committee approved the appointment of Professor R. MacGregor Dawson as editor of a new Canadian Government Series; this Series now includes ten volumes. It has maintained its momentum under the guidance of Professor J. A. Corry, who succeeded Professor Dawson, and of Professor C. B. Macpherson, who became editor of the Series in 1961. In 1949, the Social Credit in Alberta Series, edited by Professor S. D. Clark, was initiated with partial support from the Social Science Research Council of Canada under a special grant from the Rockefeller Foundation; the Series was brought to successful completion in 1959 when the tenth volume appeared.

With the building up of a strong programme of publication and of a smoothly functioning Publications Fund to support it, the Press is now turning to a major long-term contribution to scholarship. It will become the publisher of a Collected Works of John Stuart Mill. A large number of Mill's works are out of print, and some are available only in old editions; the great bulk of his essays, reviews, and newspaper articles have never been brought together and are now almost inaccessible. The value of a collected edition, in view of the increasing interest in Mill today among scholars in literature, history, philosophy, and psychology and of the lack of adequate texts with which they may work, is unquestioned. Each volume will be provided with an introduction which will comment on the relation of the work or works therein presented to the Mill canon. The texts will be presented in an attractive library format with critical apparatus wherever appropriate. This project has particular suitability for this University in view of the strong tradition of interest in nineteenth-century thought here, and in Mill in particular. It will be the responsibility of an Editorial Committee headed by Professor F. E. L. Priestley of the Department of English, University College; the textual editor for the whole edition will be Professor J. M. Robson, Department of English, Victoria College. It will thus be our privilege at Toronto to present to the world of learning a very major undertaking of Canadian scholars over a Canadian imprint.

The Scholarly Journals of the University of Toronto Press

Eleanor Harman

The idea of beginning a journal seems to have a persistent appeal to institutions and associations who feel a need for expression, or even a desire for added prestige. In university press circles, on the other hand, journals are often regarded as financial millstones hung about the neck of the sponsors. The University of Toronto Press believes that the truth lies between the two extremes. The financial responsibility is indeed heavy, but the service performed may be great, and prestige doubtless follows upon service well rendered.

The University of Toronto Press receives many requests from groups wishing to establish or obtain financial support for a journal. The need for a written statement to place before these groups had been recognized for some time when, in 1960, a report was prepared on policy and procedures of the Press, and presented to the Advisory Committee on Publications (at the same time as a report was submitted on the scholarly book publishing programme). Both reports were adopted by the Committee, and this article is based closely on the statement on the journals.

The scholarly journals publishing programme supported by the University of Toronto Press is complementary to its scholarly book publishing programme. The purpose of both is to disseminate the knowledge derived from research, and both are concerned with writing based on research that might not otherwise be adequately published. To this end, both are given substantial financial assistance by the University of Toronto Press in the form of annual grants authorized by the Board of Governors of the University. At the present time these grants exceed in total eighty thousand dollars per year, and are wholly provided by the Press itself from its other publishing, printing, and book distribution services. In 1961, over thirty thousand dollars of this grant was devoted to the support of the learned journals programme. As recently as 1947, the corresponding subsidy given to learned journals was twelve thousand dollars. The increase during the intervening years was largely directed to the improvement of what was already a major journals programme for one institution, to offsetting increases in costs of production, and to increasing the subsidies of the individual journals already supported rather than to expanding the programme to include new journals. In 1961, however, the programme was enlarged by the addition of three new journals.

This programme of publishing scholarly journals began with the *Canadian Historical Review* in 1920. The *Review* was followed by the *University of Toronto Quarterly* in 1931; the *Canadian Journal of Economics and Political Science*, published jointly with the Canadian Political Science Association, in 1934; the *University of Toronto Law Journal* in 1934; the *Canadian Journal of Psychology*, published jointly with the Canadian Psychological Association, in 1946; *The Phoenix*, the journal of the Canadian Classical Association, in 1947; and the *Canadian Journal of Mathematics*, sponsored by the Canadian Mathematical Congress, in 1949.

Three new scholarly journals came under the editorial and financial sponsorship of the Press in 1961: *The Canadian Geographer* (the Canadian Association of Geographers), the *Canadian Journal of Linguistics* (the Canadian Linguistic Association), and the *Canadian Journal of Theology* (an inter-denominational group).

The journals are published under various arrangements with respect both to editorial control and to control of finances. In some cases the total cost of publication is underwritten by the Press, in others either the Press or the learned society concerned contributes a specified amount annually, the other of these two sponsors carrying the balance. In accordance with the arrangements made for each journal, the Press supplies complete manuscript editing through its Editorial Department, design and production through its Publications Production Department, supervision of advertising through its Promotion Department, and subscription and accounting service through its business departments. Particular emphasis is placed by the Press on careful preparation of manuscripts for typesetting, and on supervision of every stage of production, to ensure that production standards are maintained.

A learned journal is usually composed of articles based on research which by reason of their length, immediacy, or significance have been considered appropriate to periodical publication.

Book reviews and bibliographies, as the tools of research, are also normally suitable for journal publication. The awareness of the scholar of the accessibility of publication in a suitable journal can lend added enthusiasm to his research, because of his confidence that he will secure adequate and reasonably prompt publication if his work merits it. The publication of scholarly journals in Canada means that the scholar need not feel his opportunity of securing publication will be limited if he chooses to work in a field particularly relating to this country.

Basic criteria for the editorial content of a scholarly journal published by the University of Toronto Press normally include the following:

1. The purpose of an academic journal is publication of research, not the dissemination of propaganda for any particular institution or any particular discipline.

2. An academic journal should fill a genuine scholarly need, and serve a public which is important, although not necessarily large.

3. A subsidized academic journal should not seek to duplicate services adequately provided by existing media, whether the latter are subsidized or not.

4. The primary purpose of an academic journal is to serve an existing academic community, not to create one, although the establishment of a journal can undoubtedly contribute a great deal to the growth of an institution or association.

5. Ephemeral news, notes, and reports of personal activities, such as might appear in a news bulletin, are not ordinarily appropriate for inclusion in a scholarly journal.

6. Any journal sponsored by University of Toronto Press is expected to maintain standards of format equivalent to those of other Press publications with respect to cover design, choice of type, selection of paper, and layout of advertisements, if any.

The financial responsibilities involved in the journal publication programme of the University of Toronto Press differ in some important respects from those involved in its book publishing programme. The main considerations to be borne in mind include the following:

1. A journal is a continuing financial responsibility which is incurred for an indefinite period and cannot be estimated in totality, even though its continuance is, of course, subject to review by the sponsoring body or bodies at all times. The expense of publishing a book, on the other hand, can be estimated, incurred, and paid, normally within a relatively short period. If funds are not available, publication of a book may be deferred or

declined, whereas a journal is not easily postponed even if funds are short. The decision to share responsibility for a new journal is therefore much more serious than the decision to publish even a very costly book.

2. The assurance of continuing support from a national association is of great assistance in maintaining a scholarly journal, and may be a considerable incentive to beginning one. This support is not only financially helpful, but important as an indication of the need for the publication.

3. The journals publishing programme and the subsidized book publishing programme of the University of Toronto Press are not in any sense competitive one with the other, but it is desirable that they should be kept in balance. Nor are they intended to be competitive with similar programmes of other Canadian institutions.

4. It is not possible, save in very unusual circumstances, to render an academic journal financially self-sustaining without altering its academic character.

5. Although the distribution of an academic journal can be improved by judicious promotion, an artificially inflated subscription list may not be beneficial in the long run to the financial health of the journal, nor to the needs it is intended to serve.

6. While the present inflationary trend continues, financial arrangements between the Press and any sponsoring institution or association will require periodic review and adjustment.

The Advisory Committee on Publications of the University of Toronto Press does not interfere with editorial policy so long as a journal continues along the broad lines on which it was established, but changes in editorship are regularly approved by the Advisory Committee.

The Editorial Function

Francess Halpenny

The editorial function as it is carried out in a university press is one of the most vital and significant aspects of the work of that institution. University press editing may only occasionally provide the high excitements of the commercial field which enliven the reminiscences of its publishers and editors: the sensing of a potential best-seller novel or work of popular history and the final discovery of its desirable shape from which the extraneous and inept have at last been pruned away. Nevertheless, the editorial responsibility in a university press has its own sober rewards and gratifying accomplishments in a succession of titles providing students with dependable and stimulating text-books, scholars with valuable information and apt discussion in a variety of special subjects, more general readers with descriptive or analytical writing which will further encourage a habit of inquiry.

The editorial contribution begins with the arrival of a large brown-paper parcel on the editor's desk, and each such parcel is opened with ever-hopeful curiosity. The manuscript, once it is acknowledged and accessioned, will usually receive at least a preliminary examination by a member of the editorial staff in whose area of interest it appears to lie. This examination will reveal the particular subject-matter under discussion and something of the kind and competence of the treatment. If the subject-matter and treatment are such as to claim the serious attention of a university press, the manuscript will be taken officially "under consideration." If it does not make a claim on that attention it will very likely be returned to the author without further activity.

A large proportion of the manuscripts submitted to any university press will be the result of years of research in specialized fields of knowledge. Adequate assessment of their content and therefore of their value as published works can only be made by fellow-scholars, although the editorial staff is usually able to make a shrewd guess about the skill with which the information has been marshalled. The assessment by carefully chosen specialist readers is therefore the next step in the process of editorial consideration, and in search of those readers an editor of a university press will often go far beyond the limits of his own campus, although he may consult his academic colleagues about the direction he should take. In the selection of readers, it is always the aim to secure a fair and objective report; at most presses, for instance, it is an unwritten rule that no member of staff of one university will be asked to assess the work of a colleague in the same university. It is always the aim, too, to move through this stage of consideration as quickly as possible, but it inevitably takes time to identify the appropriate readers and to secure their consent to act, and they will often have prior commitments which they must deal with before they can turn to the new assignment. It is a frequent experience at a university press to require readers just when every campus is engulfed in the year-end spate of essays and examinations or when every campus has almost been emptied of scholars travelling in Europe without a forwarding address. It remains, however, the conviction of all press editors that a manuscript which has taken years of devoted labour to prepare deserves the compliment of a report by the person best qualified, and that this person should be given time for reading and reflection; they must therefore do their best to instill patience in authors and at the same time conscientiousness about fulfilling their task in readers.

When favourable readers' reports have been received and the decision has been made to publish, the manuscript has to be prepared for actual production; the key action in this preparation is the careful reading by the member of the editorial staff who will see it through the press. The aim of that reading, which is guided by all the reports prepared while the manuscript was under consideration and by the general editorial rules of the press itself, is the production of "final copy" for the printer. To further that end the author will usually receive the edited manuscript back before it is sent for typesetting. He thus has an opportunity to make any late changes in fact or interpretation and to discuss with the editor the questions that he will have set down in the course of his editorial reading. With all this attention from author and editor at the manuscript stage, the proof can be handled with greater ease and speed, and corrections can be largely confined to those for typographical errors. The saving in cost alone can be considerable.

A more detailed description of the purpose of such copy-editing might well be in order; it is a feature of university press publishing and especially of the North American university presses which arouses a good deal of curiosity, and sometimes even some suspicion. Properly conceived and carried out, this editorial reading can be and should be a genuine service, to author, to reader, to printer. A manuscript is written to *communicate* its author's factual discoveries, speculations, insights; very often that communication will be assisted when the reader is caught up in a measure of the author's own emotional response to his subject. A conscientious editor endeavours to assist this communication. He has in mind as he proceeds that he is working with an arrangement of words not made by himself, an arrangement whose meaning and rhythm must be sought with persistence and sympathy. Ambiguities or obscurities or awkwardnesses may impede the communication of an author, and an editor will endeavour to suggest ways of removing these, at the same time preserving the author's wording whenever possible, or to elaborate on the difficulty in a question so that the author may solve it in new phrases of his own. Thus all editorial suggestions, whether many or few, will attempt to harmonize with the ways of expression of the author. Most authors soon realize that there is a genuine desire to be helpful behind queries which point out to them where over-familiarity with their material or haste or other factors have caused them to fail in the effect desired, and will respond to editorial questions in a matching spirit. Indeed authors who need this help the least are often the most grateful for it.

An editor has the interest of the reader especially at heart when he points out to the author for revision vague phrases, unattached pronouns (*this, that, it*), inaccurate quotations (an unforgivable sin), repetitious comment. He thinks of the reader when on the watch for minor errors of fact, and when trying to secure consistency in spelling and footnote references, for meandering in these matters will only arouse irritation in the reader and a suspicion that sloppiness in technical detail may mean sloppiness of content. "Where are we?" he will ask as he tries, for the reader, to see the structure of a paragraph, to follow the event-by-event outline of the narrative, to return from a digression to the main stream of a chapter. A great deal of attention, too, has to be given to bibliographies or references. The editor tries to see that the information these necessary tools of research contain is correct and as complete as possible within the sphere of the particular bibliography.

An editor is mindful of the requirements of the printer in the final marking-up of a manuscript to indicate the arrangement of type before it goes into production. In this aspect, of course, he is following the work of the Production Department which is responsible for the physical appearance of the book and which will have been preparing layouts and specifications about paper and binding while the book was being copy-edited. Once the book is in production, the editor will serve as an interpreter: to the author about the printing schedule and technicalities of type, and to the printer about the way various questions that arise in connection with galley or page proof are to be handled.

There are certain activities of the Editorial Department at the University of Toronto Press which deserve a special word of description. One is the long association of members of the department with the journals which the Press publishes. Most members of the Department have at least one of these journals to see through the production stage once the articles have been chosen and given a preliminary check for content by the academic editor concerned. The copy-editing of an article is a miniature of that given to a book and the purpose is identical. The associations developed with contributors to our journals have been valuable in many ways (they will often be thought of as readers of manuscripts, for example), and we are especially pleased when they are expanded into collaboration in a book-length manuscript.

The Editorial Department at this Press has also been fortunate in the fact that "the printer" it normally works with is another department of the same organization; it has thus had within easy and cordial reach the technical knowledge of various craftsmen. In turn the editorial staff provides a copy-editing service for certain specialized material from customers, chiefly institutions, who deal with the Printing Department, but whose productions do not appear over the Press's imprint.

Works which bear the imprint of this Press are given a special service by a group of editorial readers who handle proof. The permanent members of this staff develop a familiarity with the specialized and highly technical works we publish, and most of them have a knowledge of at least one language in addition to English.

It is one of the oddities of the editorial function that it is most successful when least observed. It has been well performed when the hovering pencil is least evident in the final result, and the book is clear, valid, and convincing in the procession of its words and sentences. Then author and reader are communicating to the best advantage. This is not an easy function to learn: it takes time to develop the necessary eye for technical matters, the necessary judgment to know when and how much to suggest by way of editing, the necessary skill in presenting queries to authors in order to make clear the reason for them. In a university press, the specialized nature of the list published means that editors must have a university background, often indeed including some graduate or specialist work, and must be alert to what is happening in a general way in academic circles. Despite many manuscripts that remain disappointments whatever care they receive, editors are still hopefully readers of books. As an editor in one university press has phrased it: "We admire the courage it takes to choose, deliberately, to engage in the painful process of putting words together. It is perhaps not too much to say that it is primarily *because* the editor or publisher has such respect for the difficult art of writing that he frets so much about what it is that he is publishing."

"Our Readers Report..."

Eleanor Harman

Academic authors owe a heavy debt to their fellow scholars who read and report on new manuscripts for research councils, university presses, and similar sponsors of scholarly publishing. It is no light task to read and assess four hundred pages or more of typewritten manuscript of a serious work—too often available only in the second or third carbon copy. That the task is performed so regularly and so cheerfully, and (all things considered) so promptly, is a credit to the sense of responsibility and the co-operative spirit of academic men and women.

The responsibility is an important one. The manuscript of a work requiring subsidy must be reported on favourably by one or two or three qualified readers whose opinions carry weight before being approved for publication by a university press. Many commercial presses, too, are guided by reports from readers. In addition, the councils and foundations that make collateral grants in support of publication of some scholarly works must seek the opinions of several qualified referees. It thus occasionally happens that a leading scholar is asked by more than one publishing or subsidizing agency to report upon a particular manuscript, as it passes through the various stages of consideration. This is an academic compliment to him, however unconscious it may be. The eventual publication of the work is absolutely dependent upon the verdict of the readers' reports. Granted there are other high hurdles to surmount—the financial and production problems—these are not as close to the heart of scholarly publishing as is the question of editorial acceptability.

The willingness of the academic to take on this task of assessing the manuscript can, however, be even better accounted for by his co-operative spirit than by his sense of responsibility. It might be thought that the spirit of co-operation could lead to some mutual back-scratching among academics, with the result that publishers would not be able to count on receiving disinterested opinions. Even though the academic reader knows that the publisher has pledged himself to preserve the reader's anonymity, there might be a feeling of mutual obligation that would over-balance critical judgment. After all, academic readers are often in turn academic authors, and such authors in turn are readers. However, in our experience, academic men may be rude to their wives, beat their children, and kick their dogs (for all we know), but they do maintain their academic integrity. The academic may often be prejudiced, but he is always honest, and he will not recommend a manuscript he does not think merits publication. That he may occasionally be mistaken is not as important.

One further inducement to scholars (who have a great deal of other use for their time) to contribute this service of appraising scholarly manuscripts is their own interest in the subject. A manuscript may be presumed to include new and recent work in the scholar's own field, which if it is of any value at all, he will want to read eventually when it is printed. To read it in manuscript may not be a wasted effort. He may even be prepared thereby for a request to review the book in due course for some scholarly journal.

The ability and dependability of some readers is remarkable. There is, indeed, one expert in the field of Canadian politics whose fame as a reader of manuscripts is as legendary as his personal charm. The late R. MacGregor Dawson used to declare, with his customary force and humour, that anyone who published a work in Canadian political history without first having it vetted by this reader was a qualified idiot—the reader, of course, being an equally formidable reviewer.

It can safely be said that few manuscripts are read because of the fees that are paid by publishers and other agencies for the service, although these fees should represent an honest effort to provide some financial compensation for the time and effort involved, commensurate with the resources available. On occasion, a fee is named in advance, but more often the amount is a standard one, adjusted upward when a particularly long or trying manuscript is involved, or when a reader has taken special trouble to provide a truly useful and comprehensive report.

Despite the responsible and co-operative attitude of academic men, the finding of suitable readers can be a time-consuming business. During an interesting discussion among university presses recently, it appeared that they had developed a variety of techniques for encouraging the most appropriate readers to report on manuscripts. Some telephoning and personal soliciting around the campus went on, of course. Some wrote letters; others sent telegrams; while one publisher said that he had noted that a professor summoned by Long Distance found it harder to say no. The University of Toronto Press has seldom had to resort to any extraordinary measures, perhaps because our relatively small Canadian academic community has a highly developed sense of responsibility and a strong co-operative spirit.

It is often necessary, however, to go far afield to secure a report from the most authoritative source possible. We have not often had to seek advice from scholars in China or the U.S.S.R., but our manuscripts, after they have been duly microfilmed for safety, are constantly travelling to and from readers in every quarter of the United States and several countries of Europe.

The period of time during which his manuscript is being assessed is a trying one for an author, and every effort is made by kindhearted publishers and readers to shorten it. But the securing and processing of readers' reports does take time, especially if the desired readers are located at a distance, or are temporarily away from their jobs, or if their services are sought at the time of year when they are busiest. Being human, an author would like to have his work of several years assessed in days. This is hardly ever possible, except when its deficiencies are sufficiently obvious to simplify the responsibility of reviewing it.

Scholarly publishers are divided on the matter of whether to ask an academic reader simply to read the book and report on its suitability for publication or whether to provide him with a questionnaire or report sheet, embodying some signposts, such as:

In your opinion, does this manuscript embody original scholarly research?
Do you consider that the documentation is adequate and appropriate?
Please make any general comments you wish on style.
What group or groups do you think would find this work of particular value on publication?

Those publishers who do not suggest such headings for reports take the view that academic readers know pretty well what is expected of them, and can be depended on to supply the answers to these questions without prompting. But sometimes a publisher is especially anxious to secure a complete opinion on a particular aspect of the work, and will ask direct questions.

One caution frequently given by the University of Toronto Press to its readers is to suggest that they limit comments on style, as such, to very general statements. A Press such as ours, which employs a highly qualified copy-editing staff, can well spare its academic readers the tedium of pointing out minor or even major errors in syntax. Naturally, a careless or undistinguished style is a matter for comment, but not to the extent of documenting misplaced clauses, sloppy capitalization, and so on.

The reports recommending manuscripts for publication need not be uniformly favourable; indeed, they seldom are. Agreement with the theories expounded and the views expressed is certainly not essential. In fact, it is not uncommon to receive a report such as that of the professor who said, in effect: "In my opinion, the author is working his way down a blind alley. But he is exploring it so interestingly and with such valuable insights that I think his work ought to be published." It was.

In his decision whether to recommend or not to recommend, a reader of a manuscript should, of course, weigh it as a whole. On one occasion the Press learned, long after the publication of a certain work, that one of the readers had strongly advised publication in spite of severe unexpressed reservations about the text, because it contained many excellent illustrations which he was exceedingly anxious should be made available. He was perhaps justified in making the decision that the value of the pictures outweighed the deficiencies of the text, but he should have taken the publisher into his confidence.

How long are the reports? They vary greatly, depending on the complexity of the manuscript and how much a reader has to suggest for emendation. A publisher is always grateful, however, for a report of at least moderate length—it is helpful if a reader will back up his opinion with appropriate references to the text, and details of his reasons for liking or disliking it. Frequently, a reader's report which criticizes points of structure and treatment is of enormous value in aiding the author to revise his manuscript for eventual publication, or in guiding the publisher's editor in preparing the manuscript for press. Reports can be used in such ways with great effectiveness, while still maintaining the reader's anonymity. The writer of a detailed report may very well be asked to re-appraise the manuscript when it has been revised in order to decide whether it is now ready for publication.

None of the effort put by the scholarly reader into a full and helpful report is wasted. Excellence in reporting has often made possible the publishing of books that would not otherwise have been published, and the publishing of far better books than would otherwise have been published.

The purpose of a scholarly publisher is to make available the fruits of scholarly research. He would be greatly hampered in carrying out this purpose, were it not for the fact that the great responsibility of reporting on the fruits of research is itself recognized as a special function of scholarship.

The Publications Production Department

Barbara Plewman

The Production Department, constituted as a separate department, is a comparatively recent development in the publishing world. Its functions have, of course, always had to be performed by someone or other—by the author, the editor, or the printer. If the author or editor did not have sufficient technical knowledge to specify his requirements, the printer perforce had to define these before work could proceed.

In the University of Toronto Press, the planning of production remained for many years largely in the hands of the printing plant personnel. While the editor might select the size and style of type for certain publications, he was inevitably overruled if the font were not available for use at the time. Design of title-pages, headings, etc., was generally left to the Composing Room staff. The results, though often creditable, were almost entirely unrelated to the contemporaneous advances in typography in other parts of the world.

Until the Press had developed a considerable list of publications, the need for a separate production department was not felt, and when the appointment of a Production Manager was made, the desire to add a greater degree of typographic distinction to Press publications was a major motive. The appointment of such a manager by the Press in 1946, was, indeed, the first such appointment made by a Canadian publishing house. At this time, the Press had in course of publication some fifteen or twenty books, and the Production Manager was also placed in charge of Promotion. In 1961, with an annual list of more than eighty books, the Publications Production Department includes a manager, an assistant, and an artist-designer. In addition, the typographer and the production assistant in the Printing Department are frequently given book-designing assignments.

The function of the Production Department in a publishing house is to organize and supervise the processes by which an edited manuscript is converted into a book. At its best, it is a highly imaginative and creative function, requiring in those who are charged with it a wide range of abilities, interests, and knowledge. The range is suggested by the questions which must automatically come to the mind of the Production Manager when he first examines a manuscript that is being considered for publication: To whom is this book addressed, and what format is best suited to this audience? Is it a book on which an expenditure for its appearance, beyond the minimum, can be justified as necessary to its greatest effectiveness? Is it an ephemeral work, or is it one that is likely to be in demand for many years? In other words, should the materials and design be chosen mainly to catch the eye or to wear well? How many copies should be made and what will they cost? What printing process, what typesetting method, even what type face are the logical choices in the light of the content of the manuscript? What about illustrations—are they integral, desirable, a matter of indifference? Should they take another form for the sake of economy or clarity or greater impact? A thorough scrutiny of the manuscript, together with consultation with the Editorial and Sales departments of the publishing house, will usually provide the answers to such general questions, and these answers will then comprise the framework within which future decisions about details of production will be made.

The answers of the Production Department in a university press to these questions will necessarily differ from those made in a commercial publishing house. A high proportion of our books are works of scholarship aimed at the scholarly reader, and they have, in the main, a limited popular appeal and therefore a relatively low potential in sales. There are, of course, notable exceptions, let it be admitted: we may be offered a manuscript whose content is scholarly and therefore properly in our field, but which is written with such style, lucidity, or breadth of approach, or whose author has made such a name for himself, or which is on a subject which is currently firing the public imagination to such an extent that we can expect to arouse wide interest by its publication. Might we not properly, in anticipation of this wider sale, allot a higher proportion of available funds to the production of this popular book than to the more specialized work? We might, if we were convinced that this expenditure was necessary to enable the former to make its maximum impact. But attractiveness and freshness of presentation are by no means always directly related to cost. Nor can the chief objective of a university press be to reap the highest financial return from its publishing. We have an obligation, as do all publishers, to produce the works of our authors in a form that will best meet the needs of their future readers, no matter how few. In some cases the cost of meeting these needs is tremendously high, even though it is not spent on show, as for example in the case of a book made up largely of tables and charts, which may be very expensive to reproduce yet of the utmost importance to the thesis of their author. Happily, however, an experienced Production Department can often suggest modifications in presentation that will cut down manufacturing costs with no sacrifice (in fact often an enhancement) of graphic efficiency.

Thus each manuscript must first be viewed as an entity with distinctive requirements, implicit in its contents, which must be provided for in its production. Such requirements, since they are basic and immutable, may be thought of as limiting factors. However, it is at this point that the creative imagination of the designer must take over to see the work larger than life, as it will be when it has been clothed in an appropriate format. The choices are wide—each type face has its own rhythm, its own special qualities; black type areas can make their contrast with white spaces in limitless combinations; illustrations and deco-rations, colour, texture, and even bulk contribute to the total effect. The designer with a thorough knowledge of the materials and processes of book manufacture will have little difficulty in creating for every manuscript with which he is confronted a format that is both stimulating and suitable.

By suitability is meant more than the application of a con-ventional format to a conventional subject or of eccentric typography to a new advance in thought. To be suitable, a type layout, for instance, must be workable; that is, it must compre-hend those basic limiting needs of the manuscript which have already been mentioned, it must be able to encompass all the varieties of material contained in the manuscript so that they emerge at least comprehensible and logically disposed, perhaps even freshened and illuminated by the design. In a university press the layout must, if possible, produce this desirable result at no extra cost, since, when the total number of copies to be manufactured is small (as is frequently the case with such books), the initial typesetting and engraving charges loom large in the budget.

Another measure of suitability is the extent to which the eye of the designer has been fixed on the consumer. If the latter is a scholarly reader and the book is on a subject in which he is widely read, he will usually prefer that it look not too different from other books on the subject. If he has bought the book as an addition to his library, he will want it to wear well; he will be more interested in having a sturdy binding with legible stamping on the spine than a striking jacket. An unusual disposition of the type areas, large display headings, or a new type face might irritate him. However, if the differences between the new and the old are actually subtle improvements in styling, he will probably appreciate the result without realizing that there is any change. On the other hand, the more popular works on a publisher's list (even a university press's) must compete for the attention of the general reader against all the bids from the mass media as well as those of other publishers. It is a question whether in designing his sane and sensible general books he should not dispense with attempts to attract attention by the use of more colour, more contrast, more confusion. Simplicity, orderliness, and eclecticism of design are highly appropriate to university press books, and have, for the more literate public, their own appeal.

It is a mistake, however, to equate in one's thinking the simple, the orderly, and the timeless qualities, in either the design or the production of a book, with the inexpensive. Materials and methods that contribute to long life—durable papers and cloths, gold leaf stamping, sewing that does not break away, boards that do not warp—these, obviously, are not without cost. Similarly, a well-styled interior is not achieved without the expenditure of time and effort. An important part of the work of a Production Department in any publishing house is to engage in a continuous study of styles in typesetting, to decide what styles, in general, the house should adopt for such possible ingredients of a manuscript as tables, indexes, footnotes, headings, captions to illustrations, quotations, bibliographies, preliminary pages. In a university press, where straightforward copy is the exception rather than the rule, and where the costs of typesetting and make-up are already high in relation to total production costs, the establishing of standard styles for typesetting and the careful marking of copy to conform with them are matters of the first importance. It is the business of the Production Department to act in an advisory capacity to the editorial staff whenever copy-editing involves styling for typesetting or marking proof for page make-up.

There is danger in an overcultivated respect for "standards" or a too rigid adherence to stylistic patterns, however. In the first place, it is easy, in the field of design, to mistake for the embodiment of eternal truths that which really only reflects passing fashion; it is easy to mistake what you are used to in a type face for what is legible; it is easy to feel that certain arrangements of type contribute to clarity without realizing that custom has persuaded you. The "standards" must be constantly reassessed, even for their appropriateness to the most conventional books. And where a designer has created a striking and fresh type layout for a book, a strict adherence to conventional styling in the details may be calamitous. In such a case it is essential that the design be so comprehensive that not the smallest detail is left to be decided by the copy-editor, the typesetter, or the compositor. Obviously, if the manuscript is thus completely styled in advance, a superior product will result; and the higher charges for design will at least not be supplemented by the heavy costs of indecision on the part of the typesetter or of corrections to improve appearance after typesetting has been completed.

Frequently, an unconventional design, applied to a book that is not intended for the ages, will actually result in lower costs. Why must the different ingredients of a book always be set in different sizes of type? Why is this kind of paper or that kind of cloth necessarily superior for a particular purpose? Why should the binding always be stamped in gold? What is wrong with using different colours of paper in combination with different colours of ink for certain specialized books? A book designer who does not permit himself to become dogmatic on any of these questions can often balance one cost against another. He can make up for some little extravagance in the type design by the choice of an inexpensive yet appropriate paper; the judicious arrangement of type decorations can obviate the necessity of employing an artist; if a cloth substitute is used for the binding, it can be printed all over in two colours for the price of an expensive cloth stamped on the spine only.

All these things a book designer should understand. But it is of even greater importance that the Production Department which employs him should understand them. Because it is this department that must act as custodian for the publishing house of the money to be expended on manufacture, and all facets of the cost of book production should be of interest to it. This concern to receive the utmost value for money spent is just as great in a university press as in a commercial firm, since every cent saved from one book adds to the sum that can be used to publish another.

In order to assess the probable costs of manufacture, the Publications Production Manager should know something about the relative merits of all the various printing and binding processes; in particular, which are best suited to the kind of books in which his house specializes. Most university presses, for instance, rely heavily on the letterpress process of manufacture, since for short runs where a high standard of printing in black and white is required, no other process has as yet proven itself competitive. The costs of typesetting, page make-up, plate-making, preparation of formes for the press, etc., are high, but not as high as the comparable costs in printing by offset lithography or gravure would be. These fixed initial costs can be minimized by careful planning, but they are in no way affected by the number of copies to be made; whereas costs of materials, presswork, binding, and other finishing processes vary directly with quantity. Obviously, then, these latter "running costs" gain in importance in proportion to the size of the edition of a book. Since offset and gravure presses operate at much greater speeds than letterpress machines, these processes must be borne in mind when a large run is contemplated.

Assuming, however, that letterpress is indeed the most efficient process for printing a particular book, how is it decided which method of typesetting, Monotype or Linotype, is to be employed? In general, ease of typesetting is the determining factor, although aesthetic considerations also enter into the picture. Many book designers hold Monotype faces in greater esteem than Linotype; and it is true that the individual Monotype letters do tend to fit together better, their position in a line being less rigidly controlled by the method of casting. But for straightforward copy, Monotype setting is more expensive than Linotype; and it is only when there are complications such as difficult tabular material and mathematical formulae in the copy that the use of Monotype can actually mean a saving. The publishing house that has its own printing plant is of course limited in its choice of type faces to those for which the plant has matrices. If a manuscript includes a good deal of foreign language setting, choice is even further restricted to those faces for which the special characters required are available. The selection of a type face cannot therefore be left entirely to the discretion of the book designer as distinct from the Production Department.

The subject of illustrations is one on which many chapters have been written in book production manuals, since there is a wide range in materials to be reproduced and the methods of handling them. A great many university press books have illustrations in black and white; comparatively few include colour plates, for obvious reasons. In letterpress printing, line-drawings are almost always reproduced as zinc line-cuts and included in the text, since they can be printed with equal effectiveness on most book papers. Photographs and other shaded copy, on the other hand, must be made into half-tones which require coated stock for satisfactory reproduction, and either the whole book must be printed on this paper (a solution generally deplored on both aesthetic and economic grounds) or else the half-tones must be printed separately and inserted in or wrapped around sections of the text. Half-tones in colour are almost invariably handled in the latter fashion, since it would be disproportionately costly to put large formes with considerable areas of black type several times through the press for the sake of a few pages of colour. Four-colour process plates for letterpress printing are in themselves very expensive, and if a book is to include a large number of coloured illustrations, offset lithography or gravure should be considered as the method of reproducing them, since half-tone on these plates or cylinders is relatively cheap.

The sizing of illustrations and their disposition on the page, as well as the locating of the pages of illustration within the book, are usually almost exclusively the responsibility of the Publications Production Department. But decisions about illustrations must always be made in close consultation with the editorial staff, who are in the best position to know what purpose their inclusion in the book is intended to serve.

This brings us to consideration of a subject that is important in any organization—that of communication. The Publications Production Department is very much in the middle of things, acting in the first instance as liaison between the editorial staff and the manufacturing plant, the designer, and the supplier of such services as engraving; subsequently keeping a constant watch on each book as it progresses through one stage after another, from typesetting to jacketing, to make sure that each stage of this orderly progress has been planned for well in advance and that no unforeseen costs are incurred along the way. Where an editorial staff is large in proportion to other staff, as is usually the case in a university press, the Publications Production Department rarely corresponds directly with authors; and the onus must be on the editorial staff to seek advice and assistance on production matters arising out of such correspondence as well as during copy-editing and handling of proofs. The danger in this relationship is that if the areas of responsibility are not clearly understood, appropriate steps may not be taken by the Editorial Department to ensure that the book as set in type and made up into pages corresponds as closely as it should with the book as originally planned. The production staff should have the responsibility (and be given the opportunity) to check first pages and all final proofs before printing. Where a change in specifications is desired or where corrections to proof are heavy, it is essential that the Production Department be advised, since these are matters that affect the costs, which are its proper concern.

It will readily be understood that the administrative work in a Publications Production Department will be heavy in direct proportion to the number of books being manufactured. Each book, however simple or complex it is in content, must have an estimate (and often more than one), detailed work dockets for printing, binding, and jacket, and a cost summary when work is completed. All of these the Department must either produce itself or secure, on the basis of specifications it has laid down for the particular book. The closer the final product approximates to the original as foreseen in the first specifications, the closer will be the relationship between the final cost and the original estimated cost. The Publications Production Department thus takes part in the planning of the production, guides its development, and officiates at all post mortems!

"...And to Produce *Portraits of Greatness*"

Marsh Jeanneret

The opportunity to publish and to produce *Portraits of Greatness* by Yousuf Karsh was more than a production challenge—it spelled a production dilemma. The velvety, jet black backgrounds and delicate moulding of flesh details that give Karsh portraits their unique quality had never before been faithfully reproduced in printer's ink. Yet paradoxically, Karsh portraits have been reprinted more frequently in the press, in advertising, and even in books than have those of any other photographer in history. His famous "bulldog" pose of Churchill—shot a split second after Karsh had plucked the great wartime prime minister's cigar from his mouth—became the universal trademark of British determination to fight back from the darkest days of World War II.

Nor is the Karsh portfolio any collection of ordinary personalities. For more than two decades, the Karsh shutter has been clicking before the most prominent faces in government, religion, the arts, and industry throughout the countries of the Western world. Not always has Karsh been willing to release what his camera has captured in this way, for like every real artist he is frequently displeased with his own work and destroys his negatives. But in an extraordinarily large proportion of the master prints that he has approved one can find more than a human face, for Karsh has always sought to capture what he describes as the "inward power" of the personality that he is recording. As was realized from the outset, this "inward power" is a mightily difficult quality for a printer to reproduce!

The portraitist himself set the conditions for publication of his greatest portraits in book form. "If the printed reproductions are faithful facsimiles of my own mat-finished photographic prints, you will find me very agreeable. But I must personally approve every last proof before the book goes to press!" This condition was bravely written into the publishing contracts signed by both the University of Toronto Press (which was the originating publisher) and by Thomas Nelson, who assumed the publishing responsibility outside Canada.

It was obvious from the outset that neither half-tone engravings nor offset lithography would yield the required results. The soft, jet blacks would glisten like glossies if printed from ordinary engravings on coated stock and in any event would show the ubiquitous half-tone screen, however fine it might be. And black though offset blacks can be today, they look like dull tones of gray when set beside the blacks of Yousuf Karsh. For the same reason, none of the more esoteric methods of printing, such as collotype, could be seriously considered. The delicate vignettes within the photographs precluded any method of double-printing from two sets of engravings. The only solution was sheet-fed gravure—but it would have to be of a quality that could not at the time be found in any published volume of mono-chrome reproductions. Days were spent examining art books and photographic collections of every kind; some prints served as excellent examples of desired density of background inks, others contained highlight qualities that we would have been happy to equal. But none—none whatsoever—combined all the problems present in a single Karsh portrait such as that of Hemingway, of Schweitzer, or of Einstein.

It is important to observe here that tonal values in Karsh por-traiture are sometimes present in photographic landscapes, but at the extreme ranges only. The middle tones, if present in the landscapes, seldom involve critical details. A winter landscape reproduced by sheet gravure may contain jet blacks and glisten-ing whites, and even an exciting gradation of middle tones in shadows on snow and in clouds. But the precision required to secure the pleasing effect of these middle tones in such land-scapes is simply not of the same order as that required to high-light a wisp of hair, a lower eyelid, the highlight on a lip, and the moulding of flesh detail as found in a Karsh portrait. A single hair on Albert Schweitzer's left eyebrow is two inches long and reaches almost to the moustache—and it is literally possible to count the hairs in the moustache! Is this amount of detail really important? When it is presented as detail by Karsh, it is presented for a purpose. To reduce the detail would be to change Karsh. Our duty was to reproduce the detail. And this in every aspect from subtle rounding of flesh tones to the pores in the cheeks of an aging Churchill. And although half-tone screens can put pores in any face, this was just the effect that had to be avoided.

In the end, all the Karsh portraits selected were reproduced successfully. The result was a miracle of printing production, and the miracle was wrought by the great Netherlands printing house of Joh. Enschedé en Zonen of Haarlem. But between the day the first photographs were airmailed to Holland (insured at $7,000) and the day the first copies of the finished volume arrived by air on this continent unfolds a story of production trials and tribulations not frequently experienced in the publishing profession.

Although good quality gravure work can be procured for book publication from a few sources on this continent, it is a much more widely established technique for art reproduction in Europe. Web-fed gravure does provide a highly successful means to an end for many types of periodical printing on this side of the Atlantic, but sheet-fed gravure is rarely employed here for photographic reproductions of book quality where the criterion is absolute fidelity of tonal detail and texture; certainly it has never been attempted in the United States or Canada where the complications in the way of achieving perfect monochrome facsimile are those of the majority of Karsh's photographic portraiture. Then the production department at Toronto went to work.

Paul Arthur of the National Gallery, Ottawa, was appointed production editor for the volume, to work with the printers through Barbara Plewman, Publications Production Manager for the University of Toronto Press. While production of the gravure proofs proceeded, editorial preparation of the copy went forward under the direction of Francess Halpenny, Editor of the Press.

The technical problem faced by Enschedé was nothing less than to re-Karsh the Karsh originals. In other words, the whole process from securing perfect new negatives from the positives supplied by the photographer through to etching and chroming the cylinders for mass reproduction at the level of quality of photographic prints had to be repeated in Holland. It is not surprising that the first efforts brought disappointment. The difficulties were compounded because the printer necessarily had to work from actual-size glossies, yet attain in reproduction the precise quality of a mat-finished photographic print. The processing stages between had to be worked out by experiment, much like a printer endeavouring to secure a perfect reproduction from seven-colour process plates when no progressives are available.

Experimental proofs of Hemingway, Schweitzer, and Einstein (the three most difficult portraits) reached Toronto in the late autumn of 1957. They were magnificent prints. But they were not facsimiles of the photographs being used as a standard. The trouble was fortunately traced to the quick-drying gravure ink, the blacks of which hardened to produce disconcerting highlights around detail that was otherwise remarkably fine. Enschedé went to work with alternative inks, and at last came forward with a twenty-five-year-old formula that dried to a velvety jet black, much duller than the sparkling blacks of the glossies, but of precisely the finish of the mat prints. The vignettes were exactly those of the originals, and the delicate moulding of the flesh details had not been impaired. The older, soft ink had solved the problem of securing faithful reproductions, although it created others during the machining, discussed below.

The highlights still appeared to be a little too bright, and a slight change in the stock tint in the direction of off-white was decided upon. A heavier weight of paper was considered desirable, and a search for a sheet of a more velvet-like texture began. Finally, a Héliomat paper from Office Français des Papiers Fiduciaires et Surfins of Paris, was ordered to combine the three desired qualities of tint, texture, and weight. The first mill run was to be for an edition of 14,500 copies. We had at last committed ourselves, and the order to proceed with the making of negatives and etching and chroming of cylinders was also given.

Types chosen by Paul Arthur were Spectrum for the text proper, and Dubbele Augustyn for display headings, both designed by the late Jan van Krimpen for Enschedé. As rapidly as editorial work proceeded, copy was forwarded by air mail and proofs returned and cleared against layouts prepared by the production editor. This part of the work presented few problems, although the effect of the typography in the finished book was a cause for gratification to all concerned. The gravure portraits were to fall on rectos throughout, with text on the versos facing. With the decision to use the soft ink made to the older formula, it also became necessary to avoid all machining of the sheets after the application of the gravure work. Even folding was impossible because of roller smears, as experiments quickly proved. Therefore it was decided to lithograph the text for the versos on one side of each forme before applying the delicate gravure reproductions to the rectos. Because of the impracticability of folding, thermoplastic binding was selected, to be performed on the Flexiback machine by Messrs. Proost, binders to Enschedé. (In Holland, as often elsewhere in Europe, even the largest book manufacturers commonly do not operate their own binderies.)

It quickly developed that push-button scheduling had not yet been achieved. A close liaison between Holland and Toronto was established, and numerous trans-Atlantic journeys to confer on production details were made in both directions during the months that followed. But proofs of new portraits (six portraits were run on each cylinder) repeatedly showed deviations in tonal value or printing texture from the standard of facsimile that had been set, notwithstanding the conscientious efforts of all concerned. Some defects could be repaired by hand-burnishing, but others required re-making of cylinders—a time-consuming process, and an expensive one for the manufacturers. But at no time did Enschedé remonstrate. Of course, the problem was that when a cylinder was re-made to correct a defect in one reproduction, some new flaw would present itself on another portrait.

Finally the writer flew to Holland in the spring of 1959 to meet Karsh for a final review of the problems that were being encountered. During three long days that neither of us will ever forget, we sat huddled with the management and the technical supervisors of Enschedé discussing each reproduction, being educated on how further improvements could be made and on the reasons why new cylinders might be required in certain cases and not in others. Because chroming of the cylinders is the last stage—no further retouching being possible after this is done—it became evident that insufficient allowance had been made by author and publishers for the final improvements that chroming gives the gravure reproduction. The unchromed copper cylinders tend to hold a film of ink in spite of the action of the doctor blades, thus reducing highlights and impairing to some degree other fine details. The final chroming yields a plate that produces a softer impression without loss of detail, one in which the texture of the highlights and vignettes is noticeably improved. Art directors of book publishers using this process should keep this effect in mind in their planning.

Consider the problems of production supervision surrounding just one portrait in the collection—and a similar account could be given regarding most. The first proof of the portrait of Sir Laurence Olivier was a stirring print, but not a good facsimile of the original. There was a flatness to the proof reminiscent of the slightly burned-out quality of a good picture on television. The hair appeared wiry, with the highlights in it exaggerated. Instead of a three-dimensional moulding of facial planes, the contrasts in the proof tended to be sharp, the lights a little too light and the darks a little too dark. Detail of clothing texture that had been subdued in the original had been brought out with a crispness in the proof that distracted the onlooker. The subtlety of the original had been vulgarized in the reproduction. The criticisms here described sound harsh considering the over-all excellence of the proof as a piece of printing. But the fact was that, although the proof was a good illustration, it was not a faithful reproduction. What the author described as the "gradation of highlights and the qualities of light and shade" present in the original had here been altered.

What readers of *Portraits of Greatness* will never be able to see is the contrast that exists between the first proof of the Olivier print and the reproduction that appears in the published work. By re-etching the cylinder, introducing the old gravure ink, exploiting the softening effect of the chroming process, and by superb craftsmanship in the presswork, the final result is virtually indistinguishable—even on close examination—from an original photographic print. This is a rash claim, perhaps; only those who have been able to make this comparison can appreciate how valid it is.

In the spring of 1959, Thomas Nelson, Toronto's co-publishers in the United States and Europe, presented an advance set of proofs to members of the American Library Association. As the proofs passed from hand to hand about the table, exclamations of wonderment and enthusiastic surprise were voiced by all present. Then the representative of Nelson's announced: "The proofs you have just been shown have all been rejected by the University of Toronto Press. Now let me show you the final revises!"

Little wonder that all copies of the first edition were sold out entirely to the trade in both the United States and Canada by the day of publication.

Selecting a Title

Eleanor Harman

Does the choice of title affect significantly the reception accorded an academic book? This is, of course, impossible to answer: when a work has been distributed under one title, no scientific comparison with possible sales under another title can be made. Undoubtedly it is easy to exaggerate the importance of the name with which a book has been christened. Any evaluation of its effect involves hindsight—if the book sells well, the title was probably a good one. If it sells below expectations, there is often a temptation to blame the title.

But it would be a mistake not to admit that naming a book calls for considerable creative judgment. A succinct, euphonious, graphic title holds out hope to the prospective reader that the book will be succinct, euphonious, and graphic. A touch of humour indicates that there may be touches of humour in the text. The considerations are so obviously commonsense ones that the subject would be scarcely worth discussing, were it not that a considerable number of manuscripts—and printed books— turn up with titles that seem to the publisher more of a hindrance than a help.

The ideal title, besides being short and memorable, is precisely descriptive of the book, and normally requires no sub-title for clarification or amplification. But perhaps not more than one of a dozen books receives an ideal label. Most are compromises. "What's it about?" is the frequent query when a new book is announced, despite all of the efforts that have been made to devise an adequate title.

Ambiguity is a recurrent problem. An important manuscript received last year was called initially "Canadian Securities Regulation." This apparently simple, descriptive title concealed the possibility of at least two major ambiguities. (Regulation of

Canadian securities anywhere? Regulation in Canada of securities issued anywhere?) One ambiguity at least was resolved by the change to *Securities Regulation in Canada*. On the other hand, let us admit that the title of the recent volume of Karsh portraits, *Portraits of Greatness*, has an ambiguity which is carefully intentional, although the reader may wish to reflect on what this ambiguity is.

A long title on a scholarly work may sound painfully pedantic. Think, too, of all the complexities of cataloguing and book-ordering procedure. For example, every time a single copy of the book is sold, informal abbreviation of the long title occurs; sometimes several abbreviations take place at various stages of the transaction. Absurdity, confusion, and error may result. For this reason, the author of "Growth and Seasonal Absorption of Nitrogen, Phosphorus and Potassium by *Picea glauca* (Moench) Voss Seedlings" (a precisely descriptive title) was asked to preface it with a short general title, *White Spruce Seedlings*, because of the impracticability of making a sensible abbreviation. The new general title not only saved wear and tear in the invoicing department, but was appreciated by the Promotion Department during the planning of prospectuses and advertising. The benefit was also felt by *Books in Print*, the book-trade annual which indexes by title, author, and by subjects, every book in print issued by United States publishers (and by University of Toronto Press, alone among "foreign" presses, since July 1960); by *Scholarly Books in America*, the quarterly bibliography of University Press publications issued to 160,000 academics, which also includes all U.T.P. titles; and by almost everyone who had occasion to refer to the book.

Choosing a title requires the same kind of ambivalence as making an index. In each case it is impossible to perform the task unless one has studied the work thoroughly, and then, to be successful, it is necessary to put oneself in the mental situation of someone who doesn't know the work. The title may seem splendidly appropriate to anyone who has read the book, but will it inform or attract the reader who sees it for the first time in a bookshop, on a shelf, or in a book-list or catalogue?

The descriptive title which conveys an instant meaning is undoubtedly preferable, but if it is impossible to provide a descriptive title in brief compass, the allusive or provocative title is the next best solution. This requires taste and judgment. It is fatally easy to choose a title that is meretricious, or precious, or even "just plain corny." It should be effective and memorable; otherwise even a dull descriptive label would be better. Titles based on brief quotations are often effective and appropriate, particularly when the quotation is recognizable without being banal. Northrop Frye's *Fearful Symmetry* is an excellent title, and so is W. O. Raymond's *The Infinite Moment*. Usually when the title is allusive, or consists of a quotation, the subtitle has to do the work. Sometimes, the result has an air of throwing off the disguise, e.g., *Incentive: How the Conditions of Reinforcement Affect the Performance of Rats.*

There is no copyright on titles, and the chief protection an author has against a title being borrowed by another author is the good judgment of publishers. Similarity of titles is not an important consideration in naming text-books, which are invariably known in any event by the author's name—"Dewey's Principles," "Smith's Accounting," "Jones's Trigonometry," and so forth. In books of general interest, especially if published in the same season, similarity of titles is undesirable. On a number of occasions University of Toronto Press titles have been altered while a book was in process because the name chosen was pre-empted in the same year. Sometimes, if a rather banal title was involved, the pre-empting was a relief to the editor, who was preparing for a diplomatic remonstrance.

At what point are books formally christened? About half of the books published by University of Toronto Press are issued under the titles they bore when the manuscripts were originally submitted by the author. The rest are most often named by collaboration between author and editor, when the latter has progressed far enough in editing to get the feel of the book. The method of writing down one possibility after another, with all the variations that occur, and of gradually eliminating the impossibles, is still a common as well as obvious technique. The actual title, of course, sometimes descends like lightning during this process. Finding a good title is not simple. Because of the strongly repetitive tendency in titling scholarly books, e.g., "The Rise of . . .", "A Study of . . .", "Essays in . . .", "Theory of . . .", "The Development of . . .", a powerful effort to be a little different must frequently be made. Nor are we happy as a rule about Essays in Honour of Anyone, although we have yielded—more than once.

What of the learned book which conceals its erudition under a semi-popular title? This is perhaps not a very serious crime. It brings its own punishment to the publisher in a prompt return by the bookseller, or in the failure of the scholarly reader (to whom the book is actually directed) to recognize it. But all scholarly authors and publishers of scholarly books fondly believe that a much larger public would exist for their type of book, if the public could only be induced to open the volumes and start reading. And if any encouragement can be given this respectable habit by a lively title, the end—within sensible limits—may justify the means.

The
Founding
of
DCB/DBC

George W. Brown

The Dictionary of Canadian Biography, now in active preparation at the University of Toronto Press, was made possible by
the remarkable and public-spirited bequest of a Toronto businessman, the late James Nicholson, who left the residue and bulk
of his estate to the University of Toronto for the purpose of
creating a biographical reference work for Canada of truly
national importance. Over the years Canada has had a number
of useful biographical reference works but none of them on the
scale envisaged by Mr. Nicholson. The world-famous Dictionary
of National Biography of Britain, begun in the 1880's and now
running to some seventy volumes, owed its inspiration to the
desire of an English businessman, George Smith, to do something
"of permanent value to his countrymen"; and it was this example
which inspired Mr. Nicholson when he outlined in his will the
kind of multi-volume scholarly and readable work which he had
in mind for Canada. Wisely also he provided that the income
only of the bequest should be used, though he realized that other
help would be needed as the work progressed, and thus the
Dictionary is established permanently as a major work of research and publication, with the prospect that for the period up
to the mid-twentieth century, for example, there may eventually
be eighteen to twenty volumes with perhaps 10,000 biographies
ranging in length from short notes to articles of 8,000 to 10,000
words, and that in addition there will probably be, in the master
Name File, cards and information for another 10,000 or more persons not included in the printed volumes. The Dictionary and
the Biographical Centre now being created will thus have a
biographical record running back to the earliest beginnings of
the country, and including not only the names of the great and
well known but thousands of lesser and even forgotten people

who in their own distinctive ways wove their careers into the warp and woof of Canadian life and made the Canada of today a possibility.

In 1959 arrangements were completed, with the kind co-operation of Mrs. Nicholson, to begin work on the Dictionary—July 1 was appropriately the formal date of the beginning. In the first two years foundations were laid; basic procedures created; contacts established with scholars and institutions throughout Canada and in other countries, especially the United States, Britain, and France; the contents of Volume I were determined, and assignments arranged with the nearly one hundred contributors who are writing the approximately five hundred biographical articles and notes which Volume I will contain. Of special importance in this formative period also are the arrangements, outlined below, for the creation of a French edition, *Dictionnaire Biographique du Canada*, through the co-operation of Laval University. Particularly gratifying have been the widespread interest and co-operation elicited by the Dictionary. The original announcement in 1959 brought almost 2,500 requests from all over the world for the bulletins of further information which it was planned to issue from time to time, and the response in advice and assistance since that time from scholars and institutions has been equally cordial.

One of the most important of the basic and continuing problems in the production of the Dictionary is the creation of the Master Name File from which the names to be included in the printed volumes will be chosen. Mr. Nicholson himself laid down in his will some of the general criteria of selection: the Dictionary should contain biographies not only of persons who were born and lived in Canada, but of Canadians who had careers of distinction abroad, and of persons from abroad whose activities in Canada merited their inclusion; and, finally, in all cases there must be some element of distinction in the career. Thus, Wolfe, Montcalm, Lord Durham, and many lesser persons from abroad will be included, as will Bonar Law, Aimee Semple McPherson, and many others whose careers lay outside Canada. What constitutes distinction, however, is often not easy to say, especially since no type of career is to be excluded. Like the D.N.B. of Britain the Canadian Dictionary will run the whole gamut of activities, prophets, priests, and pirates all finding a place, with the malefactors and villains, though happily outnumbered by the virtuous, lending colour to the printed page.

To build up the Name File and screen it for the final selection of names for a volume, a process of issuing Name Lists has been initiated. These lists, containing the names for a particular region or period which have up to that time been compiled by the D.C.B. staff, are sent out for examination and criticism to a selected list of experts for the region or period in question with a request for additions, corrections, opinions as to relative importance, etc. Later, when a particular volume is projected, a printed "Preliminary List of Names under Consideration" for the volume is similarly distributed. This entire process, which ensures that experts in the field are fully consulted, has been carried through for Volume I, and the replies received from over one hundred correspondents have been most helpful in providing a basis not only for the final selection of names, but for determining the lengths of articles and the possible contributors. Some idea of what is involved may be indicated by the fact that at an early stage the file for Volume I contained only about one hundred names. Later it went up to over 1,200, out of which approximately 500 have been chosen for inclusion in the volume.

The organization of volumes in the Dictionary is unusual for works of this kind, but it has certain advantages over the commoner form of organization, which is a series of interdependent volumes with biographies alphabetically arranged through the entire series. Each volume in the Canadian Dictionary will cover a period of years and will be self-contained with the biographies alphabetically arranged within the volumes. The periods covered by individual volumes will vary in length so that volumes will be approximately equal in size, the date of death determining the volume in which a biography will appear. The first volume will run up to the year 1700, the second possibly to 1740. By the second half of the nineteenth century there may perhaps be a volume per decade. It is hoped that a volume in this period may soon be projected so that the constituency of contributors and readers may be broadened as soon as possible, and with this in view intensive work on the Name File for the years 1851–1900 has been carried on for some time, including the issuing for examination of five regional lists containing some 2,500 names. Among the advantages of the period type of organization is the fact that each volume being complete in itself may be purchased or later revised without reference to a whole series of interdependent volumes appearing through a number of years. The period type of organization also has an advantage in the task of preparation, since it permits intensive work at any one time on a few selected periods, while the interdependent type of organization necessitates working at all times with equal intensity over the entire range of the national history.

Of special interest and importance is the fact that the Dictionary will be published in two editions, English and French: the *Dictionary of Canadian Biography* by the University of Toronto Press; *Dictionnaire Biographique du Canada* by Les Presses de l'Université Laval. This will break new ground since no comparable project of a similar kind in research and publication has previously taken place in Canada. At the time of the original announcement in 1959 it was stated that contributions would be accepted in either French or English and it was hoped that a French edition might also be arranged. It was clear, however, that such an edition must be suitably sponsored in French Canada. In the preliminary consideration of the possibility of a French edition, a valuable contribution was made by a French-Canadian Consultation Committee consisting of Dean Pierre Dansereau, then of the University of Montreal, Professor M. Brunet of the University of Montreal, Dr. Guy Frégault, then Professor of History at the University of Ottawa, and Professor M. Trudel of Laval University. It was on the recommendation of this committee that an approach was made to Laval University, and it is a cause of sincere congratulation that the authorities of Laval enthusiastically undertook the responsibility. The formal announcement of the French edition was made at a *lancement* in Quebec on the evening of March 10, 1961. On this occasion Mgr Vachon, the Rector of Laval University, said in part:

Ces deux éditions, l'une française et l'autre anglaise, qui seront publiées simultanément, nous apparaissent comme le symbole de la collaboration franche et entière qui doit exister dans notre pays entre les universitaires de langue française et ceux de langue anglaise.

Nous espérons que cette initiative servira d'exemple et de stimulant et qu'elle contribuera à consolider et à développer les mouvements d'échange et de bonne entente entre les deux grandes races qui constituent notre pays.

The French and English editions are to be the same in content, and it is planned that the two editions of each volume will be issued simultaneously. The work will thus be one not merely of translation, but of close collaboration at every stage of preparation. Under the supervision of Professor M. Trudel, Director of the Institute of History of Laval, who is to be the editor of the French edition, a centre of biographical research was established at Laval University shortly after the announcement of the French edition was made, and detailed arrangements soon followed for keeping up the continual consultation and flow of information now necessary between Quebec and Toronto. The collaboration involves the maintenance day by day of duplicate files, the mutual consideration of manuscripts submitted, and other problems requiring constant attention in both centres. Such a project has its difficulties, but it is a fascinating one, and worthy of every effort involved since only in such ways can the full resources of both French and English scholarship in Canada be made available to the Dictionary.

It is important also that this collaboration brings into cooperation not only researchers, writers, and editors, but the two university presses of Laval and Toronto. The project of a Dictionary of National Biography "satisfied none of the conditions of a merely commercial venture," as the preface of Britain's D.N.B. stated in the 1880's, and as Mr. Nicholson later saw equally clearly. Such a work of scholarship and research is therefore most suitably connected with a university press, and it is most appropriate that the Canadian Dictionary with its two editions should be published by two university presses representative of both French- and English-speaking Canada. The *Dictionary of Canadian Biography/Dictionnaire Biographique du Canada* is thus important not only as a work of permanent historical value but in a variety of ways as a truly significant symbol of Canada's bi-culturalism.

Publishing the Proceedings

Eleanor Harman

A striking testimonial to the degree of co-operation existing in the academic world today is the frequency with which learned congresses are attracting strong delegations from institutions and professional bodies of both Eastern and Western countries. Many of these meetings are now being held in Canada.

Whenever a Congress meets, a question arises as to how to make the Proceedings permanently available, not only to those in attendance but to scholars and research workers unable to be present. The University of Toronto Press has often been called upon to assist with such volumes of Proceedings, which require an adequate publishing service. Fortunately, the large book and journal publishing programmes of this Press have led to its developing special facilities to discharge this duty. These facilities include an unusually large and highly trained editorial and production staff, accustomed to handling academic manuscripts; a printing department equipped to produce the most technical matter in several languages when necessary; and a publishing department with world-wide distributing outlets in use at all times. The publication of a particular Proceedings may require one or all of these services.

The following observations, based on the experience of this university press, summarize a number of the considerations involved in the planning of conferences of this kind, particularly when the publication of a Proceedings is envisaged. Some of these suggestions may seem especially obvious, but they are mentioned here for the sake of completeness and because a few of them can be overlooked in the complex planning that is required for an international meeting of considerable size and importance. Many of these considerations apply also, it will be noted, to the publication of reports by conferences of any kind.

Probably the most frequent complaint made about the publication of a Proceedings is the length of time that has passed, in some countries at least, between the close of the meetings and the appearance of the volume. The value of the publication of the research obviously may be lessened if this interval is unduly extended. Careful planning in advance is essential to avoid this delay, which is generally caused either by inadequate editorial and production planning or, more rarely, by financial problems. This press has found that at present its production schedules normally improve—often by a significant factor—on the shortest schedules proposed by publishers abroad.

Planning for publication of a Proceedings should begin, of course, when invitations to actual participants in the Congress are sent out. The latter should be accompanied by detailed specifications regarding the nature, length, and form of papers to be submitted. A closing date for the submission of papers should be scheduled, any limitations necessary placed on the number and nature of illustrations, and the languages to be used for papers and abstracts specified. The closing date should be given the earliest possible announcement, and after the despatch of pre-planned reminder notices, it should be rigidly adhered to.

At this stage, the amount and method of publication should already be clearly in mind—whether a full Proceedings is to be issued, or merely a programme with abstracts, and whether book quality letterpress or simple offset reproduction from typewritten copy will be used.

Offset reproduction, in particular of scientific papers, has not been uncommon during recent years, when it has been chosen with the aim of "short-circuiting" the mechanics of production and of reducing costs by presenting the material in a purely utilitarian format. However, it requires very careful planning, and unless close co-operation is received from the contributors, can be a painful experience, and even yield no more pleasant a result. This Press is on the whole satisfied that it has recommended the use of offset only in justifiable situations. With offset, reproduction may be made either by photographing directly the typewritten papers submitted by the delegates, or after their retyping by IBM electric typewriter or similar machines. The first method is most economical, although severe concessions must be made in the finished appearance. Despite the clearest instructions provided for typing, accompanied by specimen typed pages for the guidance of authors, the papers seldom have a professional degree of uniformity. One contributor will use a light ribbon, another a dark one, and wide variations in sizes and styles of typewriting and care in execution are inevitable. Tables, references, and illustration captions often require special knowledge for their arrangement. Material prepared in this way cannot, of course, receive much technical editing. This is, therefore, not a method which this Press favours for its imprint, unless special circumstances recommend it.

Retyping by IBM or Varitype produces a better-looking volume, and it is possible to edit the text and insert the illustrations to better advantage. The savings over letterpress involved in this method may easily be over-estimated, however. If the Proceedings are to be produced with any speed, a corps of editors, artists, typists, and machines is required at the right time and in the right place. The University of Toronto Press published the 900-page Proceedings of the Congress on Nuclear Structure four weeks after the conclusion of the meetings, but this was only made possible by heroic efforts on the part of the editors and a large staff. Editing and typing began while the meetings were in progress, and were round-the-clock operations.

Letterpress reproduction remains the traditional and most generally acceptable method of issuing important Proceedings. If editing and production are precisely scheduled, there need not be an undue delay between the completion of the conference and the issuing of the volume, and the time interval has normally been measured in months only. However, if delegates carry away their papers with them, with vague promises of re-submitting them in revised form at a later date, much time may be lost in assembling the manuscript. Production cannot be finally scheduled until the day is known on which the complete manuscript will be available. Time must be allowed for the review of the papers by the Editorial Committee of the Congress, and for editorial copy-preparation by the publisher. At the University of Toronto Press, the papers for a large Congress are ordinarily handled by several experienced editors, chosen from a large full-time staff, in order to expedite this stage of production. Needless to say, copy preparation by professional editors in this way can greatly reduce the work of the Editorial Committee and its Chairman, who are usually called on only to settle queries. Professional supervision can also keep down costs by reducing the number of revisions necessary after typesetting.

As soon as the manuscript is complete, a definite schedule of production can be drawn up, with dates established for the beginning of type composition; for the delivery of galley proofs, page proofs, and revised proofs; for the beginning of presswork; and for the completion of binding and mailing of copies.

The problem of budgeting the cost of a Proceedings is not simple. The Editorial Committee has to make a considered guess as to the total number of pages, and it must be admitted that delegates frequently exceed by a considerable margin the space limits set for them. The number of copies to be printed is also a matter for deliberation. In some cases, of course, the Congress supplies a free copy of the Proceedings to each delegate attending, usually making a moderate overrun as well for general sale. It need scarcely be said that the over-all budget of the Congress must provide sufficiently for this distribution, lest the Committee find itself under a promise to publish and distribute copies, without the means to fulfil the obligation. Given the number of pages of manuscript, the proportion of illustrations, and specifications concerning the size of type and the size of type page, together with the style of binding, the printer can make a preliminary estimate of the cost of printing.

If the proceedings are published by any method, reprints must be provided. This involves estimating the costs, sending out forms to contributors, organizing the printing, invoicing, and mailing. The reprints must appear promptly, or endless correspondence with contributors ensues. The quantity of reprints required, even of abstracts, should not be underestimated. The University of Toronto Press usually offers to take over this responsibility entirely. The reprints are supplied to the authors at a break-even price, as nearly as can be estimated in advance.

If there is to be a general sale of the Proceedings the matter of distribution arises. This can be the most important consideration of all. In this connection, it should be kept in mind that many Congresses are international, and the publisher must be prepared to secure and handle sales from any part of the world. The University of Toronto Press has found its world-wide sales arrangements effective for this purpose. All the mechanics of selling—warehousing, invoicing, shipping, operation of accounts receivable—are handled by the Press, while foreign sales are procured either through its agents abroad or by bulk sales to foreign publishers. The usual means of promotion are used, advertising, circularizing, and cataloguing, and in addition, a Proceedings published by the Press is listed in *Books in Print*, the joint publishers' catalogue used by the book trade throughout North America, and in *Scholarly Books in America*, the university press quarterly which is received by some 160,000 libraries and academicians. In the course of the general advertising programme of the Press, a great deal of repetitive promotion occurs in each field, and this is essential to securing maximum sales.

Financial arrangements for publication vary greatly, depending on circumstances. However, even when Proceedings are produced for general sale, without free distribution, they usually require subsidization by the Congress in whole or in part. The volumes may run to many hundreds of pages, often of technical matter, and therefore may involve significant typesetting costs. To expect to offset these costs by sales is ordinarily optimistic. It should not be assumed, for instance, that every delegate who attends will purchase a copy or cause one to be purchased. This may be quite impossible for some foreign delegates.

The Chairman and the members of the Editorial Committee of a Congress are faced with a heavy responsibility. However, their difficulties can be minimized by careful planning and budgeting, and by conferring with the publisher at as early a stage as possible.

Selling University Press Books

Hilary S. Marshall

The function of a university press in making available the fruits of research is only half completed when a book is edited and manufactured. Then follows the job of selling it—of placing the book in the hands of the scholars, librarians, and members of the general public for whom the book was written. Often, a scholarly publisher must search out the individual customer himself, for not only is there a paucity of bookstores on the North American continent, but some of the academic publishers' wares are so limited in appeal that not many bookstores can be expected to stock them. It follows that a university press must be at least as resourceful as a commercial publisher in marketing its books. It must even be prepared to make an expenditure of time and of money which by purely commercial standards might be considered unsound. A university press must, therefore, budget this extra expenditure when planning the publication of a scholarly work.

It should be emphasized that an intelligent sales department of a university press does not try to mislead its customers concerning the scholarly nature of its books, nor to sell copies by allowing the purpose of a book to be misunderstood. Such a policy would produce an avalanche of returned copies, and seriously affect the university press's relations with booksellers and the reading public. Nevertheless, because university press books are for the most part written by scholars for others in their own field, the market is world-wide.

The planning of the promotion of a new publication begins at a very early stage. The Sales and Advertising Department of the University of Toronto Press learns of the existence of a manuscript almost as soon as it comes under consideration, thanks to the Day File system whereby copies of all outgoing letters circulate through the Press offices within hours of having been written. Editorial production schedules follow, with a monthly conference which updates the information regarding each book, and thus the promotion personnel are in constant touch with the progress of every manuscript in the hands of the editorial staff. This contact is important for many reasons, not the least of which is the necessity of administering the comprehensive promotion budget which is drawn up each year, and from which funds are allocated to the books in progress. This budget has to be flexible, of course, but the promotion cannot start until a budget has been allocated.

The main methods of promotion may be summarized under six headings: (1) review and desk copies, (2) cataloguing, (3) direct mail, (4) display advertising, (5) personal contact, (6) exhibits. Selling campaigns in Canada and the United States are conducted by the Press itself from Toronto, and the Press's representatives in the United Kingdom, on the continent of Europe, and throughout Latin America and the Far East, are provided with a steady supply of promotional materials to be used on behalf of the Press.

The Editorial Department, being most closely in touch with the spirit and content of the book, prepares a description for use in the seasonal catalogue in which it will appear. The Production Department considers the jacket design, and this will incorporate the description of the book and in many cases will also include a list of other works, carefully chosen, of interest to the purchaser.

As the delivery date of the completed book approaches, the Promotion Department prepares a detailed promotional programme. This programme, starting from the budgeted amount allowed for the book, includes the number of review copies to be sent out, and to whom they are to go; the size and general nature of the prospectus or prospectuses, and the lists to which this advertising material will be sent; the display advertising in newspapers and journals proposed for the book; and any special promotion that may have been planned.

Immediately upon publication, several routines are observed. Certain copies must be deposited with the National Library in Ottawa in accordance with statutory requirements, and others are forwarded to the Press's overseas agents and to resident sales representatives across Canada. Included in this routine is the forwarding of a copy of every book published by this Press to the Library of Congress in Washington. The latter procedure causes the book to be catalogued by the Library of Congress, and thereby brought to the attention of every major library throughout the world, together with full bibliographical information—a welcome aid to library purchasers. A copy of each book is also sent to the Association of American University Presses for listing in *Scholarly Books in America*, the university press quarterly which now has a circulation of about 160,000. Copies of the book will also be added to certain permanent book exhibits, and henceforth the title will be kept in mind for appropriate special exhibits.

In drawing up the list of recipients for review and desk copies, the author himself often provides the greatest assistance. A very complete file of scholarly journals is maintained on cards in the Promotion Department with full details of the reviewing habits of each, the address of the Literary Editor, and so forth. These journals are classified in broad groups and the lists regularly revised. Press policy with respect to desk copies for individuals, as distinguished from review copies, is to be as selective as possible, except where the book is appropriate for use as a textbook, and where a sizable adoption may be under consideration. The normal procedure is to send books "on examination," thus enabling the scholar to have the full privileges of handling and reading the book without commitment to purchase. The book is sent with an invoice, clearly stamped to show that it may be returned for full credit. If the book is selected for text adoption, all charges are cancelled by the Press on receipt of notification to this effect.

As reviews come in from the various publications, they are filed together, by title, to be referred to constantly in the course of subsequent promotional activities. It is also a normal procedure to send copies of all reviews promptly to the author.

The value of catalogues, both complete and seasonal, can hardly be exaggerated. The University of Toronto Press currently prints a total of nearly 25,000 catalogues each year (two seasonal lists and one complete list), which are distributed to senior scholars in Canada and to librarians and others who request them throughout the rest of the world. Bookstores are, of course, automatically included in such mailings. In this connection the importance of the Press's *Complete Catalogue of Books in Print* should be noted. This catalogue is combined with other publishers' catalogues in a major bibliographical reference tool published annually in the United States, which is known as the *Publishers' Trade List Annual*. The publisher of the *Annual*, using the separate publishers' catalogues, thereupon compiles a massive directory, entitled *Books in Print*, which lists every book in the *Annual* by author and by title. The inclusion of University of

Toronto Press publications in this consolidated list (it is the only non-United States publishing house so represented), has an important bearing on total sales, particularly on backlist titles.

The direct mail programme of the University of Toronto Press is quite probably the largest of any Canadian book publishing house; it is certainly the broadest in its geographical range, as it covers Canada, the United States, and overseas. Each mailing piece is designed bearing in mind the possible market, as well as the relative popularity of the book and probable effectiveness of the prospectus itself. Thus many scholarly books require a simple and dignified mailing piece, which informs the reader that the book has been published, describing it in straightforward terms together with necessary information about price and availability, and is sent to scholars in the field and perhaps also in closely related areas. On the other hand, a less specialized book with a wider potential market may justify a more striking treatment: careful selection of colour of ink or paper or both, decoration and illustration, sometimes an unconventional layout to attract the eye. All these devices, and others, are used to command the attention of the recipient. Appropriateness and effectiveness must determine the form of direct mail promotion adopted in a given instance.

In addition to the brochure which describes an individual book, the use of small catalogues or folders describing several books in the same field is an established and important part of book promotion. By this method, the public is reminded of the older books available on the same subject.

It is important to realize that this promotion is not confined to North America, much less to Canada alone. Lists have been built up of bookstores, libraries, both academic and general, and individuals, and these lists are constantly being enlarged, so that it can truthfully be said that no major academic institution, on either side of the Iron Curtain, should be wholly unaware of the publications of the Press.

The display advertising programme in newspapers and journals is becoming more and more important at the University of Toronto Press. When writing the description of a book for an advertisement, it is, of course, desirable that the copy be "slanted" towards the type of person who will read it. For example, the description of the best-selling *The Mackenzie King Record* for an advertisement in the *Globe and Mail* will differ from a description of the same book for the *Canadian Historical Review*, although both will be accurate. One advertisement is addressed to the man in the street, and by its design and appeal to the eye must arrest his attention and intrigue him, all in a very small space. The other message is addressed to a highly selective reader whose interest in the book will depend on his assurance of its authenticity and historical importance. Both advertisements must be well designed typographically, but with a different object in view.

Of display advertising it is often said that publishers place advertisements in the literary pages of newspapers to impress their fellow publishers, to appease their authors, and to encourage reviewers, but not in the hope that they will sell books! While one may not subscribe to this view in its entirety, there is no question that display advertising often is not the most efficient or most economical way of promoting the sale of a book. It is, nevertheless, an important adjunct to a more general sales campaign. Announcements in scholarly journals, on the other hand, are placed to inform a selected section of the public of the appearance of a new book in a particular field, and are most valuable.

Notwithstanding the highly academic nature of the content of many University of Toronto Press books, very generous coverage is enjoyed from radio and television. Radio reviews, an author's appearance on television or his participation in panel discussions and interviews, do not, however, "just happen." The Sales and Advertising Department must be alert to the news value of Press publications, and be in constant touch with the executives in charge of radio and television programmes.

For the less academic portion of a university publisher's list, the bookstores are the natural outlet. However, no matter how important the book, nor how evident its saleability, a bookseller is just as reluctant as any other retailer—if not more so—to commit himself to the purchase of more than a minimum of copies. Admonitions and blandishments coming through the mail, or even by such exotic means as telegrams, have little effect. A constant personal contact with booksellers is essential, so that a publisher will understand clearly what he can and cannot sell through such outlets. For this purpose the University of Toronto Press has excellent resident representatives in Vancouver, Winnipeg, Montreal, and Fredericton. It is their duty to keep in touch with the retail bookseller, to see that he is kept fully apprised of developments in the Press publishing programme as they occur. A Trade and Library Supervisor performs this function, in addition to other duties, in Ontario.

Last, but not least, an extremely important part of the book promotion programme is the display of the book itself in exhibits held at scholarly meetings, for professional groups such as librarians, and even for the general public. Every book published by the Press is exhibited between one and ten times in a year at different places and on different occasions. It is always gratifying to hear of an author's surprise and pleasure at seeing his own book exhibited at a scholarly meeting in the farthest corner of the continent. By virtue of the Press's membership in the Association of American University Presses, it is able at reasonable cost to see that its books are brought in this direct fashion to the attention of those who should be most interested in them.

A complete description of the operation of the advertising and sales arm of the Press would touch on many other activities. These would include the promotion and handling of advertising for the various Press journals, communication and co-operation with authors, and attending to the constant flow of requests for information about Press books—all of which must be handled promptly and courteously, and which, with the use of suitable promotional material, can often result in sales. But what makes the selling of academic books a constant and stimulating challenge is, in fact, the great variety of ways in which a book can be promoted, and the realization that there need never be an end to finding new ideas for advertisements and prospectuses and new avenues of sales to explore.

New Ways
in an
Old Trade

Roy Gurney

It is an interesting fact that the art of printing by letterpress remains fundamentally the same today as it was in the time of Gutenberg, or, to go even further back, in the days of the Han dynasty in China in A.D. 200. Basically, the method consists of inking a raised character and impressing it on a surface, generally paper or parchment. Gutenberg invented the type punch, by which many pieces of the same character could be made and stored for later "composition," as well as subsequent re-use. During the nineteenth century, machines were invented for setting type automatically, and many refinements made in the casting of type. Elaborate automatic printing presses have now succeeded the old hand-presses. New types of ink have been developed for use with the new equipment. Bindery operations have been mechanized. But the fundamental principle of letter-printing remains the same—impressing a raised character in ink on the surface of paper.

The general principle of book-binding, too, remains much the same, despite the mechanizing of the operations formerly done by hand. The shape of the book, the sewing of the sheets, the covering, are still fundamentally the same processes.

In some areas of the printing operation, despite all the new inventions, there has been a remarkable adherence to traditional methods for many years. This is especially noticeable in the handling of type after it has been set until the time it is placed on the bed of the press, and it is particularly in this area of production that the University of Toronto Press has introduced some innovations in the past ten years. None of these innovations has been earth-shaking, but since they are in an area which has maintained its old ways for decades, even for centuries, they are of special interest. Their economic importance is considerable since they relate to hand rather than machine operations. Collectively, these changes have revolutionized the appearance of the University of Toronto Press Composing Room in the last nine years.

Traditionally, the processes of correcting, spacing, and paging type matter were accomplished by manipulating it on an inclined "bank" resembling the old-fashioned stand-up clerk's desk of an earlier era. The individual pieces of type needed to correct errors in the typesetting, known in the industry as "sorts," were kept in small partitioned drawers under the banks. The arrangement of the compartments was designed to bring the most needed characters of the alphabet conveniently to hand, especially in common sequences encountered when everything was hand-set. Indeed, this arrangement had changed little since Gutenberg's day. Even the letters "j" and "u" still followed "y" and "z" in this arrangement because they were added to the alphabet later than the other letters. Much type is now set by machines which cast a solid slug of type for each line, and correction in this case consists of removing the lines containing the errors and inserting the corrected lines. But whether the type was set by Monotype, in single pieces for each character, or in solid slugs, it had been traditional for the compositor to carry out this process standing at his desk, or bank, working on the type held in long "galley" trays.

When the type had been corrected, it was made into pages and, by long custom, the compositor tied up each page of type with string, around the edges, and piled one page of type upon another until the job was completed. The string was unwound after the pages had been transferred to the table, or "stone," for placing in the forme, and when the pages were removed from the forme after printing, the string was wound again around the pages for storage. This procedure was known to Gutenberg, Caxton, Fust & Schaeffer, and William Lyon Mackenzie, and was hallowed by such associations—which added to the general conservatism of the printing craftsman.

The University of Toronto Press, in recent years, has changed almost all of these methods, and in so doing its Composing Room has lost much of the traditional appearance of such a department. The changes have been induced by the pressures of the varied problems involved in the kind of printing in which the Press has specialized, and suggested by ideas from printing shops in all parts of the world; we have adapted these ideas to our needs, and endeavoured to add improvements of our own.

The University of Toronto Press, a scholarly publisher, issues many books running to five hundred or more pages in length, which have all the scholarly appurtenances of set-down material, running-heads, footnotes, bibliographies, etc. The Press manufactures an edition of a scholarly journal in this style each working day. The cost of making up so many pages, with footnotes commonly at the bottom of the pages, can form a very large part of the whole cost. Methods of expediting this work are obviously very important to our Press.

The first stage in our renovation programme began with a suggestion from the editorial production department. Was it feasible to furnish page proofs from pages stored in the galley trays, and so avoid tying up the type until the pages had been finally corrected and approved for press? (Observation of advance proofs received from an American printer suggested that this might be the method already used in some plants.) Would not this reduce some of the high cost of making corrections in pages, involving—as it did—the locating, untying, and tying up again of the pages of type?

This sounds like a simple idea, but anyone who knows the complex organization of a composing room will realize the problems that immediately arose—the enormous number of galleys that would be needed; the storage space that would be required; the danger of pied type in handling Monotype pages in this manner; the objections that would be raised by editors and authors accustomed to receiving the traditional style of page proofs.

The last problem was disposed of most easily of all. The University of Toronto Press house-style allows editors and compositors, with certain reservations, to make facing pages a line short or a line long, provided that facing pages are equal. With this liberty in arrangement, it is possible to bring out pages comprising a mixture of texts of different sizes to equal length without descending to the iniquity of "carding," which is strictly forbidden by Press rules. (Newspapers, for example, commonly fill out columns by carding between lines.) Since it is the responsibility of the Editorial Department to check page lengths, the task of the editor was simplified by proofing recto and verso pages on the same galley. (By a happy coincidence, this is the same combination of pages that is locked up in sequence in the chase, and so the amount of handling done by the lock-up man was also reduced.)

The physical problems of handling and storage of the galley trays were met and disposed of one by one. An immediate question was about the real suitability of the inclined bank for making up the pages. Upon investigation, we found that some progressive printing plants were making up Linotype pages on flat tables. This sounded like a good idea for Linotype, but presented a problem with Monotype. The separate Monotype characters might fall over and become pied in a galley resting flat. Then someone suggested that the galleys be tipped slightly so that the characters would rest firmly against the galley ledge. Narrow strips of wood nailed to the table-tops would suffice for support of the tray on one side. Today, when the table-tops covered with galleys are viewed from the side in our Composing Room, they seem to resemble saw-teeth.

We found that make-up of pages was much simplified by the flat-table method. The compositor could make up forty or fifty pages all in plain view at once, and if a bad "break" developed (perhaps in matching footnotes and references, necessitating the reworking of a number of pages to take back lines or bring lines forward), the problem and its solution were much easier to visualize.

The cost of making corrections in page proofs was reduced, since the tying and untying of the type pages was eliminated. This is one of the reasons (the other is the return of edited manuscript to the author for O.K. before typesetting) why the average cost of "Author's Alterations" has been sharply reduced at the University of Toronto Press.

The correction of Monotype material is also done on the flat tables, with their saw-tooth arrangement, but the hand compositor's "sorts" (the characters he uses in making corrections) are kept in a quite different manner from the traditional method. In Gutenberg's day, and for hundreds of years afterwards, the hand compositor was chiefly occupied in the original setting of the copy. This work is now done by machine, and the hand compositor's chief function is to make corrections, or to make by hand any complicated adjustments of the type which are impossible by machine—today, very few. It is, therefore, no longer necessary for the hand compositor's sorts to be arranged so that the most frequently used sequences of characters are "in line"; instead the emphasis is on having an abundance of characters of all kinds readily at hand for correcting. This need for numbers of characters in correcting was felt very acutely at University of Toronto Press. The fact that we specialize in setting mathematical and chemical formulae and foreign languages has trebled and quadrupled the number of characters in everyday use.

The old method of storing characters in drawers had to be investigated and another method of holding "sorts" devised. The method that seemed to hold most promise was that devised by Robert H. Roy, formerly director of research for Waverley Press, Baltimore, and now Dean of Engineering at Johns Hopkins University. Mr. Roy, examining the problem from the engineering standpoint, had pointed out that 30 per cent of the existing boxes in the standard, traditional arrangement represented wasted space by reason of the manner in which the type was placed. He proved that by piling the type characters neatly side by side 30 per cent more type could be added to the boxes. Furthermore, differing sizes of boxes were no longer needed. He devised a small plastic box about one-inch in all dimensions that could be filled semi-automatically on the Monotype caster. By having the boxes made in different colours, arrangements could be invented for the individual compositor's ease in handling. The lower case Roman letters, for example, could be in boxes of one colour, the capital letters in another, italic letters in a third, figures in a fourth, and so on.

The University of Toronto Press first became interested in the plastic boxes through observing them in use at Waverley Press in 1953. The boxes had, however, been manufactured especially for Waverley, and it would have been extremely expensive to arrange for special manufacture of them for our Press. But the idea was kept very much in mind, and two years later it was learned during a visit to our plant of Mr. Christopher Pitman of the Pitman Press, Bath, England, that the cases were in use in his plant. He had bought the moulds in the United States and had the boxes made for him in England. He had now sold the moulds to a British firm which was willing to manufacture them generally for the printing trade. Our order was placed at once. Four weeks later, our Plant Superintendent received a call from a Toronto manufacturer's agent, located scant blocks away from the University of Toronto Press, wanting to know "what in tarnation are the Rob Roy cases I'm supposed to be selling to the University of Toronto Press?" The Rob Roy cases are now in full use, and it is calculated that 300 per cent more characters can be stored in the former total space.

When the galleys of type have been set and corrected, they must be proofed and stored, and this was a major problem at the University Press, which had to make the fullest use possible of every inch of space available. The problem was solved by designing, and having made to our order, mobile galley racks, which are stored under the flat tables. When page proofs are made, the rack containing 45 galleys or 90 pages is wheeled to the proof press, proofs pulled, and the rack wheeled back to storage space. Each rack is shifted by means of a small skid truck; the racks might have been equipped with wheels, but this cost was felt to be unnecessary. Instead of the rows of banks which formerly stood in the Composing Room, we see flat-top tables, with six mobile galley racks beneath each. Incidentally, all the tables and racks were constructed to our design in the Carpenter's Shop of the Superintendent's Department, University of Toronto.

The cost of making page proofs has also been halved, since two pages are now proofed at one time instead of one. The inserting of running-heads is simplified by setting in type all the left-hand running-heads (normally consisting of the book title or an abbreviation of it) and inserting them as the pages are first made up on the galleys. The right-hand running-heads (normally consisting of abbreviations of the chapter-titles) are provided by the editor, set in type, and inserted along with the page corrections made in the galley trays.

When the page proofs have been O.K.'d for press, the pages of type must be removed from the galley trays and placed in the formes on the stone, or make-up table. Until a few years ago, the pages of type used to arrive at the stone individually wound round with string. This string was carefully removed by the make-up man, who rewound it into neat little skeins for re-use when the pages were removed from the forme. The first stage in improvement of methods at this point was to give the make-up man a new spool of string, and remind him that it was cheaper for him to throw away the old string than to spend the time rewinding it. (So strongly ingrained was this habit of conserving string, however, that at one stage the foreman was reduced to going round at night and removing surreptitiously all the little skeins. But in the end the idea took hold.)

String has now been entirely eliminated on Linotype pages, and replaced by a pressure-sensitive tape about .005 inches thick. Once the tape has been wound around the page, it need never be removed except when type is to be "killed" and the metal thrown into the scrap barrel for remelting.

The taped pages of type are now stacked in mobile page racks, each of which carries twelve stacks of 16 pages each (16 pages being one complete forme or section for the average book). Moreover, the pages are stacked in the order in which the make-up man will place them in the printing forme. When the printing has been completed, and the forme returned to the stone for breaking up, the pages (if they are to be held) are returned to the page rack in the same order. On this rack they can then be transported conveniently to the "morgue" (where type that is being held for reprinting is stored). When the schedule of work in the University printing plant requires the transporting of type to a trade house for printing, the former hazards surrounding shipment of the type are overcome by these versatile mobile page racks. Similarly, when the Press has typesetting done by trade houses, the transfer of the type to our plant can be accomplished easily, safely, and efficiently.

It should be pointed out, however, that today the University Press tries to hold as little type as possible. The development of offset printing has made re-runs by this method as efficient in many cases as reprinting by type, when the extra handling and cost of holding of metal (tying up both capital and storage space) is taken into account. Moreover, many books might be held in type but never reprinted. Since much of the expense of such handling for storage is incurred *at the time the type is taken from the forme* and transferred to the morgue, the Press now regularly "kills" the type directly from the stone. This practice of destroying the type of the first 32 pages of a book when another three or four hundred pages remain to be printed impresses some printers as being almost foolhardy. However, the Press has calculated the risk, and has demonstrated that for the extremely few occasions when an error occurs of importance enough to cause a reprint of a "killed" forme, it is cheaper to reprint by offset, or even reset the type, than to use up man-hours and tie up equipment by holding type of every job until each job is wholly completed.

The kind of book for which the Press normally holds type is a text-book or reference work which it expects to issue in revised editions over an extended period. While it is possible to reprint such works by offset, the cost of typesetting, proofing, pasting-in, and cutting up and repasting pages, makes the revision by letterpress comparatively reasonable in cost and much more flexible in handling. Books which contain half-tone illustrations, fitted into the text, are also better held in type if a reprint is contemplated. The original prints of the photographs have a habit of disappearing after being returned to the author or institution, and many people, especially scientists, are still not satisfied with the sharpness of offset reproduction of photographs even when the original prints are available.

Possibly the University of Toronto Press's most startling contribution to printing procedures has been in the field of proofreading. The proofreader of years ago—indeed the proofreader of yesterday—would be dumbfounded if he could walk into the proofroom at the University of Toronto Press and observe the readers at work, each equipped with his own tape-recorder, microphone, and head-phones. This method of proofreading, introduced by the Press in 1960, is beginning to spread across the continent. Since the principle and the techniques involved are discussed in detail in another article in this book, they will not be developed here.

A word about the handling of the corrections made by the proofreaders may, however, be of interest. Since time immemorial, typesetters have groaned at the incomprehensibility and waywardness of copy, and authors have complained about the errors introduced into their perfect text by printers. At the University of Toronto Press, the proofreader is the key man in this situation. When inconsistent copy arrives in the University printing plant, it is normally given first to the Head Reader for styling; he may, if necessary, communicate directly with the customer. If it is a piece of printing that recurs, he jots down notes on the style, and thus has a record of what is wanted when the job comes in again. This check by the Head Reader is not a long process, but a quick overview; its purpose is not to edit the copy but to reduce the problems for the compositor and to eliminate the most obvious alterations.

Inevitably, alterations do occur. All corrected lines in Linotype are, however, proofread by the Press before they are inserted into the pages, thus virtually eliminating that most annoying type of error—when one correction is made in a line only to introduce another. The proofreading department is often assigned another duty—that of separating author's corrections from the literal errors made by the compositor, so that the proper charge may be made for the former. In addition, the proofroom examines the first galley when any new job is begun, to make sure that no wrong fonts, damaged matrices, or misinterpretation of style are apparent, and to ensure against the likelihood of cumulative errors of all kinds.

Passing from the Composing Room to the Pressroom, we note a very recent development in the preparation of the type forme on the press for printing—"makeready" as it is known to the trade. Throughout the history of letterpress printing, the pressman has been faced with the problem of adjusting the pressure between the type forme and the paper stock on which it is printed. This problem is observed most acutely in the printing of illustrations reproduced by half-tone engravings. It may be approached in two ways: first, by making all elements of the forme the ideal height (.9184 inches), and second, by providing extra pressure in the packing of the cylinder of the printing press. The levelling of the forme has been largely achieved by modern equipment such as block levellers, metal bases, and type gauges. To provide extra pressure with the correct variations across the face of the forme by packing the cylinder is another and more difficult matter.

The packing is mainly for the purpose of building up the tone. In printing an illustration, a solid area of black coming in contact with paper necessarily has one-half the pressure in pounds per square inch that a 50 per cent tone has, unless this pressure correction occurs. Extra impression has to be applied to solids to balance, compensate, or equalize the pressure on other areas of the engraving. Hand-cut and mechanical overlays have been used with varying degrees of success. Indeed, hand-cut overlays, packed around the cylinder, have been the common method of correcting pressure on half-tones in Canada.

Recently, however, the University of Toronto Press has installed the 3M Makeready system. It consists of two elements: a plastic-coated heat-activated material, and an exposure unit. After the forme of type is on the press and positioned, a proof of the forme is made directly on the plastic-coated sheet, which is then passed through the exposure unit. The carbon black in the ink absorbs infrared light rapidly from the exposure unit and is transformed into heat energy, which causes the plastic-coated sheet to swell. The amount of heat, and the amount of swelling, depend on the amount of carbon black in the ink. Since there is more carbon black in the solids and less in the lighter tones, the makeready sheet expands to match. The exposed sheet is now thicker in the black areas of the half-tone, and thinner in the light areas. It can then be placed as a whole unit in the packing of the press cylinder to register with the forme and the press is immediately ready to print.

In the bindery of the Printing Department, new equipment has been added or substituted to keep production in line with modern needs. Since the plant now produces so many scholarly journals, a modern Brehmer covering machine attaches paper covers in a fraction of the time formerly required to apply these by hand.

The library rebinding section provides a great contrast in methods and equipment to former days. Since 1910, the bindery has been binding and rebinding books, both for our own University and for other libraries and other customers. Despite constant study of methods, the increasing cost of hand labour had begun to make the work uneconomic, and the problem of meeting delivery schedules increased. About ten years ago, the Press began to plan for reorganization of this part of its operation. The Library Binding Institute, with headquarters in Boston, was consulted, and the rebinding standards of the Institute adopted.

The Press counts in all 41 steps that may be required to rebind a volume. All old glue, old sewing, or wire staples have to be removed. Advertisements and covers may have to be discarded, indexes brought forward to the front, repairs made, "fold-ins" protected. The sections are oversewn, and endpapers made from strong fibre are applied. The standard covering is Library Buckram with the proper thread count, colour fast, and scuff resistant. Stamping on the spine must be plain and legible and accurate in detail.

The equipment purchased to speed delivery includes, besides the oversewing machine, a P.I.E. Automatic Rounder and Backer, an ingenious hydraulic machine that can take one or two hundred library books of varying sizes and thicknesses and round and back them one after the other, adjusting its own setting electronically. The old bookbinder's press used for so many years, with its heavy screw and brassbound boards, has disappeared to be replaced by a small hydraulic press with heated platens and a controlled "dwell" which can be varied from five to twelve seconds. This machine, using modern heat-set resin glues, makes it possible to press a book in seconds where only a few years ago it had to remain in the screw press for twelve to twenty-four hours.

No longer does the binder set brass type line by line, each line in its own pallet and combined in a larger holder to stamp one book, the type having to be redistributed and recombined before the next book is stamped. Today the type is set on a type-setting machine, the Ludlow, which casts display-size lines in solid slugs. The type is proofread and corrected if necessary, and the type delivered to the stamper. A patented holder spaces out the lines almost automatically, and after stamping, the slug is immediately put aside for remelting.

The schedule for library rebindings at the University Press to-day is two weeks for any book or list of books. This schedule has been set to meet the need of the librarian, who must have his research journals back on the library shelves as promptly as possible if the requirements of scholars and researchers are to be met.

For those libraries which do not have a complete procedure of their own, the Press has designed standard rebinding instruction forms, self-addressed labels, and many other aids to streamline the operation. Recently, the Press has stocked, for the convenience of librarians, "neutral" paper (acid-free) for the making of simple protective folders for rare maps and similar material. This paper is imported from the United States where it is used by many famous libraries, as well as by the restoration departments of the Toronto Public Libraries and the University of Toronto Library.

It will be noted that the purpose behind the introduction of these new ways into an old trade is to put more work through in the same time with the same effort. This increases the capacity of the plant without adding to it physically, improves the efficiency of its operation, and adds to the security of its employees at all levels and in all departments. The co-operation of the staff throughout has been excellent. Both men and management are constantly searching for new ideas: trade journals are read carefully, and visits are made to other printing plants at every opportunity. In return, the University of Toronto Press extends warm hospitality to any trade or university printer who wishes to inspect our plant. In the competition with rising costs, the Press and all other printers are partners.

As we look into the future, it may well be that new developments now being perfected will one day replace letterpress printing as we know it at the University Press. We ourselves will be alert but not impulsive, we hope, when the time comes for such changes to be made. Beyond that, we leave the problem to our capable successors as the University of Toronto Press continues down the years.

The Printing of Mathematics

Roy Gurney

The history of mathematical composition at the University of Toronto Press begins with the installation of the first Monotype keyboard and caster in 1910. The purpose of adding this equipment to the Linotype already installed was to facilitate the typesetting of mathematical examination papers.

The first major mathematical publication undertaken by the Press was the *Proceedings of the Pacific Congress of Mathematics* in 1924–28. Even today, this 1941-page work, in two volumes, would be a major publishing project, equivalent in length and complexity to about ten or twelve issues of the *Canadian Journal of Mathematics*; for a plant the size of the Press at that period, it was an impressive accomplishment.

The volume of mathematical and technical typesetting at the Press gradually increased. In 1941, the Mathematical Expositions Series was begun, with the publication of Professor G. de B. Robinson's *The Foundations of Geometry*. Other volumes followed, and in 1949 the *Canadian Journal of Mathematics* was launched. This journal, which publishes articles on advanced mathematical research, regularly includes a large proportion of complicated formula matter.

By 1950, the capabilities of the University Press in mathematical typesetting were being severely taxed. Only one of the machinist operators really possessed the requisite skill, and he was becoming advanced in years (he finally retired from the Press after reaching the age of eighty). There were two or three highly skilled hand compositors capable of making up the complicated formulae, but their available time was overloaded, and it was becoming very difficult to train apprentices in this difficult craft. To find Canadian craftsmen in the industry who had this skill was virtually impossible. Another problem was, of course, the increasingly high cost of the hand operations involved in the composition of technical material. Labour cost had already become the major item in any printing job, and this was reflected strongly in the cost sheets for mathematical works being produced.

At this point, Mr. V. C. Collett, Plant Superintendent of the Press in 1950, visited the Graphic Arts Exposition in Chicago, and there met Mr. Wade Patten of the Lanston Monotype Company. Mr. Patten had evolved a system for setting mathematical formulae on the keyboard. Although he had been working on his system for a number of years, he had been hindered by an unexpired patent on an essential element in his scheme, and by lack of interest on the part of his employers. Only one or two printing houses in the United States had even experimented with the system up to this time.

The University of Toronto Press was in need of new equipment, both casters and keyboards, and the decision was made in the next few months to purchase this machinery, together with the special keybars, keybanks, and stop bars, special matrices, and auxiliary equipment on the casters, needed for the installation of the Patten system. In October of 1951, the equipment arrived.

The events of the next few months are seared in the memories of those who were connected with the Composing Room of the University Press at that time. The Press experienced the difficulties of all pioneers. Although the fundamental principle of Mr. Patten's system was sound (as attested by its acceptance and development today by the Monotype Corporation in Great Britain), there were innumerable major and minor problems that developed when it was put into actual use. The Press had at this time the invaluable counsel of Professor G. de B. Robinson, Managing Editor of the *Canadian Journal of Mathematics*, who spent many hours in the Composing Room and casting room, considering mathematical and mechanical problems with equal concentration and aptitude. In the end, every technical problem was overcome.

The following description of the mechanical typesetting of formulae is drawn largely from the *Author's Manual* prepared by Professor Robinson for the guidance of authors submitting mathematical papers to the *Canadian Journal of Mathematics*.

In the older method of Monotype composition of formulae each character of 10-point type was cast on a body 12 points in depth, and while this allowed for the setting of indices by machine, it precluded the superposition of superscripts and subscripts except by expensive hand work. To overcome this and other difficulties the new system allows for the casting of characters on 6-point bodies. With this added flexibility it is possible to build up even the most complicated formulae on the machine and avoid almost all the handwork which formerly led to delays and inaccuracies. The accompanying illustration shows the positions of the characters on the type bodies. All of the type is put in place mechanically except the large signs, brackets, and braces.

For the benefit of those unfamiliar with Monotype setting we briefly describe the mechanical processes involved. The edited manuscript is handed to the operator of a keyboard much like that of a large typewriter. When a given key is pressed a certain combination of holes is punched in a paper tape. After the whole manuscript is keyboarded the tape is taken to a second machine called the caster. In this machine the code punched on the paper tape is translated into a pair of co-ordinates which locate a matrix or mould of the required symbol which is brought into position over a nozzle through which comes molten metal under pressure, thus casting the symbol. The metal hardens very rapidly and the symbol on its metal "body" is moved over into a tray which gradually builds up lines of type to the length of a "galley." After the necessary changes are made by hand the metal is inked and a proof can be pulled.

It should be noted in the accompanying illustration that characters frequently "overhang" and are supported on neighbouring bodies. That such support is adequate and no breakage of type occurs is a tribute to the accuracy with which the machinery is made. The need for such supporting bodies, usually blanks, places a considerable added strain on the keyboard operator who must visualize the arrangement of the symbols as they will issue from the caster.

$$\int_{-\infty}^{\infty} H_n^2(x)e^{-2x^2}\, dx = \int_{-\infty}^{\infty}\left[\frac{d^n}{dx^n}\,e^{-x^2}\right]^2 dx$$

To set the formula, the compositor works through the formula four times; hence this method is known as "four-line" formula setting. As will be noted from the illustration, in the first line the compositor casts the necessary superior indices, together with blanks of the correct set size to accord with the succeeding lines of the formula—so far as keyboard motions are concerned, the compositor actually sets the entire formula four times, but the use of the "delete" key results in casting the spaces necessary instead of the characters. The metal spaces set in the position of the integral, bracket, or brace are removed by hand, and the signs substituted.

The four-line formula system introduced into Great Britain recently makes use of the Patten system, with, however, one difference. If the formula illustrated is examined closely, it will be observed that the denominator line is not solid, but consists of a series of tiny broken dashes. These dashes are cast separately, except when a first order superior in the denominator is required; in this case they are actually cut on the same matrix as the superior. In the British system the denominator lines still have to be inserted by hand, as apparently the British mathematicians have been unwilling to accept the broken denominator line. In our opinion, the breaks are unobservable if equipment and workmanship are good.

The first setback the Press encountered in the installation of the new system was the discovery that the superscripts and subscripts of the second order were too small—they were about $3\frac{1}{2}$ points. To Mr. Patten, concerned with the mechanical problem, they seemed adequate, but they proved unacceptable to mathematicians. The first order indices were about $4\frac{1}{4}$ points as designed by Mr. Patten, and it was necessary first of all to increase their size. Communication with the Lanston Monotype Company in Philadelphia on this complicated problem having proved almost useless by ordinary means, the new Plant Superintendent, Mr. Roy Gurney, finally sent his chief operator, who was also a skilled caster-man, by airplane to Philadelphia with the mats in his pocket, where he exchanged them for regular 8-point superior and inferior. And then the Monotype Company took the punches that were used for the original first order and re-punched a brand-new set of matrices of the second order. The first order were now about $5\frac{1}{2}$ points in size, and the second order $4\frac{1}{4}$ points. These sizes proved to be acceptable, especially after improvements were made in the quality of paper and of ink used for mathematical publications.

At the time the change was made in the sizes of the indices, a good deal of material in proof was in the hands of customers, who subsequently returned it for correcting. At the same time, setting of material using the new sizes was proceeding. For a period of about six or seven months, the Press was receiving proofs, some of which had to be corrected in one set of sizes, and some in the other. The day when the final proofs of material set in the small sizes went to press was a happy day; no tears were shed as the old sorts were thrown away, despite the investment they represented.

Another simple change ended a weakness that cost the Press much in time and money. In the original installation, Mr. Patten had insisted that the secret of his system was the setting of all matter in 10 set. The Press was equipped with 10 point 21E, which is normally $10\frac{1}{4}$ set or $10\frac{1}{2}$ set, that is, the standard quad of type in this size is $10\frac{1}{4}$ or $10\frac{1}{2}$ points wide. Mr. Patten had not fully appreciated the fact that since all except the simplest formulae are, when using this system, normally separated from the text and set on the special formula keyboard, it really did not matter whether the text portion were 10 set or not. Since $10\frac{1}{4}$-set characters were used regularly in correcting other Monotype text in the plant, both 10 and $10\frac{1}{4}$ sorts were in the cases, and inevitably the sorts became confused in the correcting, with consequent irregular letter-spacing. When the situation became clear, all the 10-set sorts for correcting text matter were removed from the cases and destroyed.

The Press has had to have many symbols specially punched for use with the system, and a very considerable number specially drawn. The integral sign is a case in point. None of the existing integral signs available from the Monotype Company could be fitted into the system to produce a result that was fully acceptable to the mathematicians at the University of Toronto. The main problem was that the regular integral signs were set at an angle, which resulted in the limit sign at the bottom being placed too far away from the integral. It could not be brought closer except by cutting it in by hand. A new drawing was therefore executed, with the sign in a more vertical position, and a special punch made. This particular symbol cost the University Press about $98.00. (A regular symbol costs about 98 cents.) It was only the first of many special signs that have been made over the years.

To expedite the problem of correcting with a wide assortment of mats, the routine was introduced of tapping (on the machine) the special mats three, four, or five times, so that each galley of material with special inserts had extra symbols at the bottom of the galley for correcting. The use of the Rob Roy cases (as described in an earlier article) has, of course, greatly simplified the problem of providing and using the large number of sorts required for correcting this complex work.

Training operators on the system was, of course, a problem. Although Mr. Patten came to Toronto and spent some days here explaining his method, much of it had to be worked out and revised in the light of experience. To develop proficiency in four-line formula setting requires, even today, special skill, and it is perhaps not strange that in those early days a few operators, having more or less conquered the problem themselves, tended to develop prima donna characteristics. However, as the system was mastered by competent new operators, the operation became progressively more routine. The Monotype School in Great Britain now gives instruction in the system; although their method, while based on ours, is slightly different, this training is helpful. Incidentally, our own experience in developing the system has been heavily drawn on in Great Britain, and many exchange visits have taken place during recent years.

The mechanical setting of formulae reduces the subsequent hand work and yields a "tighter" appearance in the finished product. The time and cost of setting are thus both materially reduced. First and second order indices, being set in place mechanically, are aligned with an accuracy almost impossible to achieve with hand work. But as with other printing, the co-operation of the author and of the editor is essential to the success of the method. It is desirable for the author to understand in a general way the mechanics of the system, so that he will at once appreciate the benefits it confers in accurate alignment and other details, and be prepared to accept such editing of his manuscript as may be required to make the fullest use of the mechanical system, for example, the separation of formulae from text. Fortunately, however, since the introduction of formulae into text lines would result in the spreading of the lines, with resultant uneven spacing of the page, the separation of text and formula is as a rule an aesthetic improvement. Some expressions which might be presented with a denominator line do still remain in the text, but these are handled with the solidus, and this preserves the normal line spacing.

One essential in the editorial preparation of the copy for the compositor is, therefore, the separation from the text of formula material, which is to be "displayed." The editor also has another duty, which may be performed for him in the Composing Room, and that is the examination of the manuscript for the purpose of listing the special characters which occur in it. Even the capacity of the 15/17 matrix cases is sometimes strained to accommodate all the characters required in intricate copy, and the case must be made up very carefully to include all the necessary signs. Each mathematical manuscript carries with it into the Composing Room a sheet on which the special characters are listed, to guide the operator and the caster-man in planning the machine composition and casting.

While the early stages of the installation of this system were undoubtedly trying for the Press, a great deal of satisfaction is felt in having pioneered in the development of this fascinating and unusual technique in an ancient craft.

A New Technique in Proofreading

Marsh Jeanneret

The art of proofreading is as old as the craft of printing from moveable type. But while composition, printing, and binding continue to be areas of never-ending technical innovation, developments in the technique of proofreading have been so few as to leave it an almost static art. Nevertheless, proofreading remains a vital link in the printing production chain between manuscript and competently published work. The finest crafts-manship is vulnerable to proofreading which is less than perfect; but intelligent and conscientious proofreading, at every level of production, can do much to ensure technical as well as literal perfection of the printed product.

A new technique in proofreading was conceived, tested, and introduced by the University of Toronto Press during 1960–61. We believe that it is likely to enjoy a very general application in the graphic arts field, and that it also possesses many potential advantages for authors dealing with proof and manuscript, as well as with transcriptions of source materials of all kinds.

Before describing this new technique, let us note the traditional methods used in proofreading in normal composing-room practice as well as by authors and editors dealing with their manuscript material at the proof stage. There are two basic tech-niques, each possessing its own advantages and disadvantages. The older, and perhaps still more generally used (especially by authors working alone), is the comparative method. This in-volves direct comparison of proof with manuscript, phrase by phrase or line by line. The more technical or complex the editorial content, the more frequently the comparative method is resorted to, even by skilled readers in a composing room. It is probably rare for an author to use any other technique.

The second time-honoured method is to "read in pairs." Under this system, a "copy-holder" reads the manuscript aloud to the "proofreader"—the more skilled of the pair, incidentally. (The proofreader should *never* read to the copy-holder.) This technique of dual reading has significant advantages over the comparative method, and a few shortcomings. Dual reading is more rapid (in total man-hours) and of even greater importance, it is much more accurate. The whole attention of the skilled proofreader is concentrated, without interruption, on the proof before him. Errors of interpretation of manuscript committed by the machine compositor would have to be duplicated by the copy-holder not to be noted by the proofreader (it is for this reason that the direction of reading must invariably be from the former to the latter). The proofreader working with a copy-holder may devote a larger proportion of his attention to the many other proofreading responsibilities, including important but subtle typographical details such as ligatures, spacing, leading, height and quality of metal, indents, "rivers," and correctness of fonts. He may, if he is competent to do so, even raise queries about syntax or content for further review by editor and author, although this will not be his primary responsibility.

Shortcomings in the dual method of proofreading include the fact that the proofreader must frequently resort to comparative checks against the manuscript, especially in highly technical and tabular matter. From an administrative standpoint, continuous organization of readers in pairs, handling of interruptions of all kinds, and the need for the comparative checks just mentioned, spell inefficiencies and resulting loss of competitive position in production costs. It is also true that the proofreader is denied the advantage of continuously "visualizing" the original manuscript as he reads the proof. While he thus gains in ability to concentrate his attention on the type, he is not allowed to become acquainted with the manuscript's "personality." This may seem like a subtle disadvantage. But there is a false finality about print, and it is unfortunate that the qualified proofreader may be subjected to its influence by the dual method. It was well described by J. Donald Adams when he referred to the peculiar protection accorded the manuscript by the typesetter in these words: "Let us not forget, either, the strange mesmerism of print; that curious, and so often spurious, authority that seems automatically to invest a page of type, even when it resembles closely a plate of tripe."

The new University of Toronto Press method of proofreading exploits the advantages of both the traditional procedures just described *by making the proofreader his own copy-holder*. Under this new system, use is made of a tape recorder of the office type, modified to permit instantaneous switching between the dictating and playback functions. The total of man-hours required for proofreading by the new technique is significantly less than by either of the old methods. Most important, however, the accuracy of communication between copy-holder and proofreader is brought close to perfection, for they are the same person.

In the present experiment, various makes of dictating machines were tested, and compared from the standpoints of simplicity of operation, quality of recording, initial cost and probable maintenance and depreciation costs, cost of materials, ease of "spotting" positions during use, space required for equipment, re-winding time in the case of tape recorders, and ease of transfer between "dictate" and "listen" positions. In the end the Philips Dictating machine was selected,* and an important modification proposed by the University of Toronto Press was immediately incorporated by the manufacturers. This involved insertion of a dictate-play-back switch in the wiring, to permit change-over of functions without necessity of attaching and removing plugs.

A special advantage of the Philips machine is that the tape is carried in a plastic magazine, and may be recorded on both edges, i.e., the magazine may be "flopped" at the end of the tape (approximately 30 minutes), and dictation continued on the other edge of the tape. When this is complete, no re-winding is necessary before play-back, which may begin either immediately or after additional magazines have been loaded with copy. References to break-off points in the manuscript, as well as other advice to the "reader" can be dictated at the time of reading the original copy.

Mr. R. Allen, Head Reader in the University of Toronto Press Printing Plant, makes these observations: "By acting as one's copy-holder and then as reader, a unity, a 'one-ness,' is achieved which cannot be equalled by one person reading to another; when dictating the copy you not only record the spoken word, you also memorize such things as name-spellings, style, indents, etc. The two operations are thus fused and a greater accuracy is obtained. . . . By having the copy at hand as you 'listen,' quick checks can be made on any doubtful points, and if you feel there is anything which could be more accurately or more conveniently compared, you tell yourself at the dictating stage to 'compare equation 11 on folio 13.'"

*This machine is sold under the trade name, Norelco, in the United States.

As Mr. Allen points out, the ability of the proofreader to visualize the copy as he listens to it being read exploits the advantages of both the comparative and the dual reading methods. Another significant advantage, involving a lessening rather than an increase in strain for the proof-reader, is summed up by Mr. Allen as follows: "While it is often necessary to control the speed at which a copy-holder reads in order to interpret accurately what he or she is saying, experience of two of us using the machines shows that you may read as fast as you are able and still comfortably follow yourself when 'listening back.' "

The possible usefulness of techniques and equipment similar to the above is obviously not confined to the composing rooms of printing departments. Publishing and editorial offices, libraries, and museums, where accuracy of either typescript or proof can thus be checked, even against original sources, should be able to utilize the reading system described here. The use of the technique at the University of Toronto Press shows that "electronic copy-holding" possesses advantages ranging from increased accuracy to increased output and lessening of an operator's fatigue. Since this technique was first announced by University of Toronto Press in April, 1960, many references to it have been made in printing trade journals, and it has been the subject of demonstration and discussion at proofreading workshops. Mr. Allen has received a large volume of correspondence and requests for articles from North America and overseas. He has remained enthusiastic about the technique and neatly summed up its advantages when answering a question from the Assistant Director recently concerning the possible monotony of "reading in pairs alone." His reply was: "Copy-holding is always a little monotonous. But with this system, listening to the copy-holder read back is *pure pleasure!*"

The Scheduling of Printing

Roy Gurney

The scheduling of production is an important function in most manufacturing plants today. Indeed, it is unthinkable that a modern factory using production-line techniques could operate without the most careful and detailed scheduling. Nevertheless, in the printing industry there are many plants which have very rough-and-ready systems of scheduling, if any at all. Some of these firms have indeed sought to install improved systems, but have abandoned them as unworkable.

The reason for such failures is that printing does not easily lend itself to normal production-line engineering. It is almost always custom work. Except for newspapers and large periodical printing firms, there are usually as many customers to serve as there are jobs in process, and each buyer of printing establishes his own specifications. He chooses the type, the paper, the ink; he decides how many copies he wants, and when he wants them. On the other hand, the manufacturer of washing-machines, or typewriters, turns out identical products, making as many as he thinks he can sell. If each washing-machine had to be devised in a fashion different from every other washing-machine manufactured in the same plant, his problem of scheduling production would be much more complex. Instead, it is rendered even more simple by reason of the fact that a merchandise manufacturer often delivers to his own warehouse—he does not have to produce a particular washing-machine on a particular day, as the printer must normally do with each printing job.

Since printing work is custom work, the purchaser must participate fully in the process. Just as a buyer of custom-tailored clothing must try on the garment to see if it fits before production can go forward, a buyer of printing commonly checks his proofs at various stages.

Even though manufacturing of printing is to be distinguished from manufacturing of other merchandise, efficiency demands that the plant continue to receive a full flow of other work even when a particular project is halted for proofreading by the customer. By one means or another, all the separate printing jobs, with their different specifications, their different delivery times, and their different customers, must be fitted into an efficient production plan. This can best be brought about by a fully developed printing scheduling system, but it must be a scheduling system which everyone understands and in which everyone has confidence.

As already noted, some kinds of printing plants can be operated without detailed scheduling of operations. But this is possible only because the repetitive nature of their product, and the deadlines to which it is manufactured, permit informal operation scheduling in co-operation with close delivery scheduling. It is also true that where the ratio of number of impressions to number of jobs is high, less detailed scheduling is required. But whenever versatility of production is combined with short average press runs, the need for the closest possible planning of operation times is urgent.

There are shops, of course, which have complex printing problems and yet "get by" because of the experience and capability—one might almost say artfulness—of the supervising staff. Their extreme dependence on the personal factor is precisely the reason that such plants too often also flounder in a state of continuing crisis, saved only by the ingenuity of the supervisors who are responsible for the turmoil. It may be true that in such shops "the wheel that squeaks the loudest gets the grease," and the customer who deals with them may find that to get delivery when he wants it he must keep nagging—nagging for his galleys, nagging for his page proofs, and probably shouting for his final delivery. The customer may even learn to ask for his job a week before he really needs it; and the printer may learn that he can deliver a week late. The customer is virtually encouraged to make unreasonable demands upon the printer: to deliver copy late, to hold proofs for further correction while precious hours or days go by, and then to demand a delivery date which is impossible in a printing plant, no matter how much other work is postponed or put aside.

While the ability to deliver printing jobs on time is the most obvious benefit of scheduling from the customer's point of view, the benefit to the printing plant itself is even more significant. It bears directly on plant efficiency. The whole morale of a manufacturing plant depends on the security of employment, and it is the duty of management to ensure this necessary continuity of operation by maintaining the plant's competitive position in the industry.

Efficient operation of a printing plant does not necessarily mean the speeding-up of individual operations. A good, steady, average output is more desirable, coupled with optimum utilization of the plant capacity. Scheduling is not expected to increase the pace of the craftsmen; a good typesetter is able to set only a certain number of ems per hour, even though he constantly seeks to improve his skill. Scheduling, however, puts operations in step with one another; it organizes the separate processes rather than speeds them. Non-chargeable time is the greatest item of expense in a printing plant—wages and costs of material are actually secondary considerations. Non-chargeable time caused by waiting for a job to appear from another department, for ink and paper stock to be ready when needed, and for machines to be prepared for use, can be almost wholly eliminated by efficient management. To reduce one of the chief causes of non-chargeable time—failure of proofs to arrive from the customer—detailed planning of operations is of great assistance.

A printing plant may appear to be overloaded with work, with its employees maintaining a breathless pace, and yet not be utilizing more than 75 per cent of the available work hours. The University of Toronto Press printing plant, in which operations are closely scheduled, commonly works to 90 per cent of its scheduled work hours. Since the schedule board is loaded many weeks in advance with a large proportion of the actual work ahead, it is possible to make adjustments among the different departments of the production machine, so that all may reach their full potential output.

The operations schedule also indicates well in advance when it will be efficient for the plant to mount a night shift; it makes clear when a rush of work is only a short-term emergency and when it represents an actual increase in volume over an extended period. A regular night shift, working to capacity, helps to reduce costs of plant operation, since depreciation, heating, and other fixed expenses are incurred on a time, rather than a production, basis. Overtime, on the other hand, is costly, and if it persists in a plant running in the day time only, if often indicates either that the several plant departments are not in step, or that a night shift is justified. Operations scheduling provides the answer to the question that is raised in this way.

It would seem that any system of time-tabling that would

enable a printer to maintain cordial relations with all customers, to keep his craftsmen fully and efficiently employed, and to maintain his plant running nearly to capacity, should be greeted with enthusiasm and adopted at once. Unfortunately, it is not simple to introduce such a system, to operate it, or to secure the co-operation of customers that is necessary for its success. The University of Toronto Press set up its first formal scheduling board in 1954, and the resulting system is still being refined, although it is now several years since any senior member of the staff suggested that the Press could survive without it. The scheduling programme enables the plant to produce on time a vast number of scholarly books, academic journals, calendars, programmes, tickets, envelopes, library rebindings, and other work. At any one moment, up to five hundred separate jobs may be in process in the plant. Obviously, so versatile a programme is made possible only by a complete operations schedule, and at the same time imposes a tremendous strain on that schedule. But its success has won the confidence of the printing staff, as well as a truly amazing degree of co-operation from customers. The system, while not perfect, has indeed been described as the most advanced of its kind in any printing plant in North America, but it continues to be further developed.

Scheduling, as the customer of the University of Toronto Press sees it, consists of a series of assigned dates. He is told that if he submits his copy on one date, galley proofs will be returned on another date; he will be expected to return them by a specified date; and so on until delivery is completed on an assigned date. Scheduling, from the point of view of the printer, is something like a railway system. A train on the track has to go from one place to another in a prescribed number of units of time, minutes, or hours, or days. It has to leave one station exactly on the time scheduled, and arrive at its scheduled destination on the minute. (It is perhaps an unusual kind of train in that it can only travel at one speed.) As it proceeds from one destination to another, it passes various other trains of many types: fast trains leading in the opposite direction, slow freights going in the same direction as itself. It stops at stations along the way to pick up freight in some places, to discharge it in others. If the freight is not ready at the station to be picked up when the train arrives, it must be rescheduled on the next available train. Perhaps the freight arrived at the station three minutes late. But that three minutes may cost a twenty-four-hour delay if space cannot be secured on another train until a day later. When the customer appreciates fully that failure to return proofs on the scheduled date may mean a delay that is considerably longer than the actual time lost, because the job must now find another place in the schedule, he will make a stronger effort in the future to return the proofs on time, or if this is impossible, will understand why deliveries must sometimes be rescheduled.

The scheduling of printing must take account of many variables, some of which are indeed difficult to forecast; indeed, it cannot be as precise as the freight-handling analogy. The estimator can calculate closely the amount of material to be set by machine, and the time it will take. But when it is set, it will probably contain errors—some of the kind that an expert typist might make, others perhaps caused by mechanical factors or deficiencies in the machine. The material must be proofread in the plant and returned to the machine compositor to have the incorrect lines reset. Thus the simplest job, even if its complexity and size are well known, has to go on the same machine twice at different time intervals. Multiply this by dozens of jobs of different complexities, where the advance information as to size, date of arrival, quality of manuscript, etc., is vague, in doubt, or even unknown, and it will be seen how much experience and understanding is needed to make printing scheduling a success.

The scheduling board at the University of Toronto Press is basically a flexible Gantt Chart using a series of horizontal slots, each slot allocated to a single shift of one machine. The whole board is made up of movable sections accommodating the total possible productive hours of regular shifts in two calendar weeks. The movable sections slide laterally, right to left, on a rail. To load the board it is necessary to determine as accurately as possible the numbers of hours necessary to process each phase of production, for example the number of hours on the press, the number of hours on the folders, and so on. These hours are converted to strips of card on which the hours are marked off in exact relationship to the lengths of the slots on the board; a strip cut to 35 hours in length corresponds exactly to a week on the board. When all the strips have been prepared, that is, cut to the right length with the job details entered on each slip, they are loaded in the appropriate time areas against the appropriate machines. There each strip stays until that particular phase of production is completed—or cancelled. As the days progress, an imaginary vertical line representing the actual date moves across the board from left to right, and a daily check is made of all work showing on the left side of the line. All jobs to the left of the line should in theory be completed and all cards removed;

any that remain are problems. To solve these problems, extra shifts may be allocated, or overtime may be scheduled, or outside assistance secured from one of the commercial trade houses—any device may be utilized to keep the "time-table in agreement with the calendar." At the end of each two-week period one section of the board is cleared of all cards and the section is removed from the rail. The section of the board just removed is then fitted with new dates and is reintroduced at the far right. To be useful, the board must cover a considerable period; the University of Toronto Press schedules 26 weeks into the future at all times.

Loading the board is, however, only part of the task. Communication of the information being generated must be prompt, complete, and effective. All important "due" dates for each job are entered in a day book or diary and an individual schedule sheet made out to accompany the job through the shop. (Remember that several hundred jobs are in the plant at one time.) Production scheduling requires that everyone whom it affects —and these are many—be fully informed, and constantly informed. It has to tell the customer when he should be expecting his job, and so a card is issued immediately the job is scheduled; a card is sent when an agreed deadline may be missed by the customer; and a sticker is attached to each enclosure of proofs reminding the recipient of their scheduled date for return. A card is also sent to inform him of new dates, when a delay in such return has required rescheduling.

A vital part of the scheduling procedure takes the form of a meeting of supervisory staff of the printing plant during the morning of every working day. The principal agenda of this meeting is a detailed review of all jobs scheduled for further processing in each department during the day at hand. If emergency measures must be taken to meet a schedule, they are decided on at this meeting. Each supervisor and foreman makes his contribution to the solution. Thus it is a group decision, not merely an order from management, that might involve undesirable reshuffling of the day's operations.

Before a cycle of scheduling can begin, it is, of course, necessary for the scheduling officer to receive the most complete available specifications for each job, i.e., numbers of pages, size of press run, and the complexity of typesetting. Normally this information will be derived from the Estimating Department, which will already have completely "manufactured" the work in question, albeit in blue-print only.

However, there is more than one approach to scheduling a

printing assignment. A customer may require a production by a deadline. If the reasons are good, and if the deadline is feasible (in the opinion of the scheduling officer), the Press may have made an undertaking accordingly. A programme of events for an international congress is a possible example. The actual "copy" may still be undelivered, but a detailed manufacturing schedule is nonetheless required as part of the planning committee's agenda. And so the scheduling officer draws up a pilot schedule. It is sent to the customer's committee for its approval or comments. The various dates for each operation may then have to be worked back and forth several times, always keeping in mind both the problems of the customer and the limitations of time available for manufacture. Finally a firm schedule evolves that may be acceptable to the customer and practical for the printer; it is this schedule that is confirmed in writing. When fortune smiles, the "copy" may even be available by this stage.

If the specifications of a production are simply not available at the time a schedule must be assigned, the scheduling officer again builds a "man-of-straw," but in this case he *reserves* approximate times in the relevant areas on the scheduling board. Clearly, only a certain percentage of future production time can safely be encumbered in this way. However, experience indicates that as long as the proportion of "reserved" but unscheduled time is low, it is advantageous to introduce it in the planning.

What happens to a small job, too small to occupy a space on the board? It is included *en bloc* with many other small productions. Even so, specific dates relative to each such job are entered in the day book, and must be brought up for review in the meeting of plant supervisors on the due date.

If the customer does not ask for a definite delivery date, an arbitrary date is assigned. As soon as the work order has been received, a work docket is opened, the schedule drawn up and a postcard despatched to the customer acquainting him with the delivery schedules. One of two things may then occur; either the customer accepts the date, or he rejects it and notifies the originator of the card (the scheduling officer) that an earlier delivery is desirable. If possible, the request is granted; if impossible, the scheduling officer is at least well documented for his further discussions with the customer! It is essential that both printer and customer know their respective responsibilities in advance, because the customer is so definitely a part of the production team. He is almost always understanding, and always can be helpful, if he is furnished with all the facts.

As mentioned at the outset, it is possible to conduct a printing business without using a detailed operations scheduling system. However, for the University of Toronto Press, at this stage of its history, scheduling has provided the solution to many serious problems. Beyond the fact that it has made it possible to increase over-all productivity, and to produce virtually every job within the time limits promised, it has vastly improved relations with customers. Indeed, customer-printer goodwill is mutual. When the staff knows that a customer has given up evenings and week-ends to maintain a tight schedule, co-operation in arranging overtime or special scheduling is willingly given. Detailed scheduling of operations has become the basis of an effective and happy partnership.

Typography and Communication

Harold Kurschenska

The purpose of each piece of printing is communication, and to this end all of the various typographical skills are subservient. Typographical design is simply a vehicle for words, and it can emphasize or subdue, shout or whisper, the meaning of what it carries. Its power may vary. A particular design concept may be effective one year, and ineffective in the succeeding year; as each new approach via design to our changing society appears, art directors and designers are quick to follow the leader, and soon the redundance of similar patterns in print outmodes the idea. Since communication through design is so changing, the designer must also remain fluid and original.

There is no reason why a poster should look like every other poster. On the contrary, it may be that the less it resembles a conventional poster, the greater the number of people who will be induced to read it. Needless to say, however, it should be attractive as well as original. People may stop to look at advertising matter and read it just because it is attractively produced. This result is the contribution of the typographer or artist who designed the work, since copy cannot speak for itself until attention is attracted to it by some element or elements in the design. A typographer, therefore, seeks to render his design in a form both attractive and original, so that he may achieve maximum communication.

The success of good design depends upon good copy, which can be responded to. Its aim and audience must be assessed, and the feelings it has evoked must be analyzed. From his experience in dealing with intricate subtleties in type, a typographer can match the mood of the copy in type, sometimes in the manner of a jazz musician improvising upon his instrument.

To the typographer there is a definite and inevitable relation between form and content. Because this is highly personal to him, no two typographical designs are the same. The relation of form to form and of form to content has been studied by Klee, Mondrian, the Dadaists, and the Gestalt psychologists, but so far we know little more about the creative process than we did before they undertook their researches. But the typographer is ever aware that content may take on "significant form" (or, sometimes, alas, fail to take it on) at his pencil's end.

The anatomy or study of the structure of a typographical design may well look like the doodles of an executive on a telephone pad, but from these rough sketches, relations to space and content of a given area develop into patterns, which the designer then renders in actual size letterforms on the layout pad, fixing exact length of line and position to facilitate interpretation by the compositor.

The typographical designer is to be distinguished from the graphic designer chiefly in one respect. Both may design ephemera—posters, notices, letterheads, and so forth—but the typographer uses primarily letterforms and type ornaments, and his work correspondingly tends to reflect a literary quality, whereas the work of the graphic designer tends to emphasize pictorial elements. The most interesting feature of the typographer's work will be the arrangement of the letterforms; in the graphic designer's layout, the picture or drawing is the foremost element.

In the typographical design, too, the "craft" element is almost as important as the layout. The hand-compositor who carries out the design makes an essential contribution. The fitting of the characters in a displayed line may involve very delicate adjustments, including, for example, the hand-cutting of some of the type. Close spacing of the lines of text, done by a skilful compositor, will hold each line together as a legible unit, both increasing the legibility and giving depth of colour to the block of type. And, needless to say, the skill of the pressman in giving sharpness and even colour through many impressions is equally necessary. With good craftsmanship in composition and press-work, a very simple conventional design may be acceptable; without it, an original design may "fall apart."

Since his work is with words and with letterforms, book design provides a particularly interesting challenge to a typographer. Here his fancy must range within quite clearly defined limits. Despite the novelties of such designers as Merle Armitage, despite the tall, narrow, thin books, and the short, wide, thick books, a book is a book is a book. Since about the fourth century of the Christian era, books have looked like books. They have had leaves following leaves, with the sequence of recto, verso, recto, verso. The leaves have been bound on the left-hand side, and the pages flipped from the right. The margins of the type-pages are not as generous as they used to be, but despite occasional attempts to drop all the type to the bottom of the page, and variations in the traditional proportion of the margins, the margins themselves remain. When all the libraries of the world have become so crowded that books are preserved only on film, then the book as we know it may cease to be, just as the scrolls of the ancients were replaced by the folded book. But in the meantime there is a good case for following the traditional format in its main essentials. Since the purpose of the book is communication, it follows that the communication will be more direct if it is in an accustomed form. The typographer seeks to heighten that communication, not to interrupt it. However, he can do a great deal to enhance the appeal of the book as a "package," and to deepen the communication.

The traditional order of the contents—half-title, title-page, copyright, preface, contents, half-title, text, appendices, index —is a convenient framework within which to work, and still permits many variations by the typographer. That each of these items of contents should begin on a right-hand page is also a sensible and practical rule. But such rules are not the laws of the Medes and the Persians. Granted that a designer who did not know the rules would produce a hodge-podge disturbing to the reader, a designer who knows the rules, and consciously breaks some of them, can achieve freshness and vary his impact. He can convey an additional message, such as that the book is uncon-ventional, humorous, romantic, poetic—although a typographer tries generally to be more subtle than this in relating form to content. However, if a scholar engaged on research were to find every book he looked into differently arranged in order of material, he would not be grateful to the designers for such vagaries. (Such variations we do, of course, encounter in older books, some of which, for example, were first issued serially, with the result that the Contents pages were printed at the end.)

The book jacket is the most striking feature of book design, and the university press designer is aware that his jackets will stand on the shelves and in display windows alongside the products of commercial publishers. They must, therefore, be able to command attention. However, the university press book will, generally, have a longer life than the commercial book; hence the typographer must design jackets which reflect fashion but are not completely of it. The same principle applies to the format generally, which, needless to say, should relate to the jacket and the jacket to it.

While the design of commercial printing and of scholarly books may seem worlds apart, the typographer for the University of Toronto Press must maintain his footing in both worlds. The University Press is publisher to the University of books, and printer of its ephemera. The typographer must endeavour to see that all printing which might or might not bear the imprint of the University meets a high standard, and that the Press's own publications and ephemera have a personality all their own.

The desire to set a certain typographical standard for all work emanating from the University Press is not always easy to reconcile with the desire to please all members of staff and departments who send work to the Press. The typographer himself does not think that every design he creates is as successful as every other one, no matter how hard he has tried. It is inevitable that some of his ideas will not appeal to those for whom they are planned. The only solution is to try again. In this process, a customer can be of most help if he will make clear at the outset which elements, or which words, of his text he wishes to emphasize most strongly, for emphasis is decidedly the customer's affair. The over-all impression which he wishes to create is also his affair—whether it is to be sober and dignified, graceful and gay, unconventional, or even bizarre. But a customer is of least help to the designer when he suggests such alterations as the position of lines on the page, the spacing between them, and so on, since these details can seldom be changed without damaging the design. It is better to start over with a fresh design entirely.

Contrary to an impression one often finds, it is not really difficult to "sell" unconventional typographic design, even in a conservative University community. The average person, although he may profess not to admire "modern" art, probably does not realize how his eye has actually become accustomed to it through advertising, interior decoration, and architecture. He instinctively though unconsciously recognizes the "freshness" of modern design. A more valid reason why it may at times be difficult to "sell" a new design for, say, the cover of a journal or a university calendar, is chiefly the appeal of familiarity—like the natural human affection for an old hat. Needless to say, of course, the individual or committee which is hard to "sell" for this reason is not usually thinking of the design in the same way that the typographer does—that is, as a piece of printing which must first secure the attention of the reader, and then communicate a particular message strongly to him. In some cases, doubtless, it is better to adhere to the time-honoured design, but it is better only when the chooser is thinking first of the impact on the audience, not of his personal preference.

Because of his varied responsibilities, a typographer for a university press is thus probably midway between an expert in quality control and a corporate image-maker. Fortunately, he does not work alone. His work can only be successfully accomplished if he is able to work in harmony with the editor, the compositor, the pressman, and the binder. As Earle Birney said in *Canadian Art*, four years ago: "What we need most of all on this continent is that voluntary, even spontaneous, working-together of independent artists . . . the joint-work of author and artist . . . inspired by the same feeling, approaching the same subject matter from opposite directions."

Printing Cost and Costing Printing

J. G. Garden

The printing plant of the University of Toronto Press is a complex organization, comprising a staff of about one hundred individuals—highly skilled craftsmen for the most part—and dozens of machines, all engaged in different operations. Every day (and night) many different printing orders, large and small, are in process in the plant, and many different machines and different workers share in the production of most of these jobs. How are all the costs of manufacture sorted out, so that each job is charged with precisely the work and materials which have been put into it, and how are expenses such as heat and light and depreciation of equipment and building charged so that each little or big printing job bears its equitable share?

Whenever the University of Toronto Press completes a piece of printing, the total cost of the job must be computed and an invoice rendered to the customer. Several hundred orders, large and small, are in process at any one time. Frequently, a firm estimate of the cost is made before work is begun, and the invoice is then issued to the customer in the amount quoted—but it is still necessary that the true cost be determined, among other reasons to know how accurate the estimate has been and to provide a basis for future estimating. But where does the estimator secure the data on which to base his quotations? An estimate is based on known production averages for particular equipment and operations, compiled in the Cost Department. In this department the daily work records of the Printing Department are brought together and processed, so that each printing job may be exactly costed, and the Plant Superintendent, the Foreman, the Estimator, and others concerned, be provided with the data for efficient management of the plant.

Each Printing Department employee is responsible for keeping an exact record of the time which he spends upon each printing job during each working day. In practice, these time reports are broken down into six-minute periods (tenths of an hour) which can be more easily processed in the Accounting Department. All plant wages are paid on the basis of the hours worked according to these records; in addition, the time each employee devotes to an individual printing job is totalled up, costed at the "hour rate" which has been set for each operation, and added to the value of materials to make up the total cost of the job. The hour rate which is set for each operation—typesetting, presswork, binding, etc.—includes not only the wages paid to the employee, but all other items of true cost. For convenience, "cost centres" are established, comprising groups of men, or machines, doing similar work. Each cost centre is assigned an hour rate calculated to "recover" all wages of associated operators, as well as an equitable share of the over-all plant overhead—wages, supplies, repairs, type-metal costs, light, heat, water, gas, power, salaries of supervisors, depreciation and insurance, shipping and stores, office expenses, and general administration. The total of all these items over any period constitutes the expense of operating the cost centre, and by dividing this total cost by the number of man-hours or machine-hours likely to be utilized during such a period, we arrive at the hour rate that must be charged for the cost centre.

In preparing an estimate, the Estimator is in effect drawing up in advance the cost sheet for the finished job—to be checked for accuracy when the work is done! He enters the time which he expects each operation to take, and multiplies it by the cost centre rate for that operation. He plans each step of the production, working out the hours and the costs accordingly. He calculates the amount of paper, ink, engravings or other materials that will be required and adds in these items.

In "costing a docket," i.e., in working out the final cost of the printing job, the cost clerk performs the same operations, but this time there are available the actual records of the times spent, of the materials requisitioned, and invoices for engravings and other items supplied from outside the printing plant. If the plant is operating efficiently, and if the estimating is being carefully done, estimate and final costs should be close. For obvious competitive reasons, the Estimator cannot afford to err in *either* direction.

To establish valid cost centre rates is a serious and complex accounting responsibility. Each cost centre has in any period a possible number of available productive hours. But not all this time will be chargeable. Time is required for oiling and cleaning the machines, and time is required for scheduled breaks, etc. More important, the loss of time through imbalance of "loading" of the cost centres must be pre-calculated. And continuous checking is necessary to make sure that non-chargeable time does not vary from budgeted limits, and thus invalidate the hour rates being used.

The element of accident may upset the best calculations. An operator may be indisposed, or may not have received clear instructions; one of the machines may not be functioning perfectly; humidity in the atmosphere may be high, slowing down the running of a press; paper stock may be too cold or dry, also slowing down the presswork. Therefore a constant check must be kept on output or productivity, through the Cost Department's records, in order that the hour rates in use shall remain true "cost recovery" rates, and also remain competitive.

The Cost Department is not actually a separate department of the Press, but a sub-department of both the Printing Department and the Accounting Department, and its responsibility is to guide the factory management. The Cost Department itself dictates no policies and makes no recommendations regarding technical matters. But it does report to the plant the results of operations, and points out deviations from anticipated results. In this way the plant can determine if it is operating efficiently, and on a competitive basis with other printing establishments producing a similar quantity and kind of printing. The best proof that such results are being achieved is to be found in the load of work of all kinds scheduled for the months ahead. All such work is produced at the lowest rates available in the Greater Toronto area, having regard for comparable quality and service.

The University of Toronto Press has also applied cost accounting methods to the preparatory stages of printing manufacture—copy-editing, design, and production. These costs are frequently handled by publishers as part of their general overhead, but the method of accounting used by the Press has some definite advantages.

By this method, each editor fills in a time-sheet very similar to that used by the craftsmen of the plant. The categories of work are, of course, different, consisting of work charged directly to book manufacturing dockets, work charged to learned journals dockets, time spent in appraisal of manuscripts, etc. Hour rates for editing, for production, and for design, are struck, based on the actual cost of operating the departments concerned, including salaries and all related overhead costs, and the individual books or pieces of printing are charged directly with the amount of time spent on them. By this means the true cost of editing and designing each publication is known at the time the total production costs are computed. As a result, the Editorial Department, for example, is able to sell editing services on a true cost basis to outside institutions whose publications are issued by the Press. Since each department—editorial, production, or design—is handled as a separate cost centre, the decision to add a new editor or a new typographer depends entirely on whether sufficient chargeable work is available to occupy the new member of staff—if so, the inclusion of an assistant tends to lower the average overhead per employee and to decrease the over-all departmental rate, rather than to increase it.

The completion of the time sheets is not too arduous a task, since editorial work, in particular, tends to be concentrated on a minimum number of projects at one time. The Editor is able to forecast roughly on the basis of previous records what time will be needed for the various manuscripts, and what the personnel requirements of the Editorial Department will be. However, no "firm" quotations are given for editorial costs on any manuscript, because of the impossibility of predicting what difficulties may be encountered, although the "guesstimates" are often remarkably close.

While the idea of subjecting creative activities such as editing, production, and design, to a mechanical cost accounting system may seem at first glance inappropriate or restrictive, in actual practice it has transformed the University of Toronto Press Editorial Department from a "loss" department—to be deplored, but accepted as an inevitable necessity—to a department which "breaks even" on its costs, and enjoys the esteem of its sister departments not only for its intellectual prestige but for the business-like methods by which it is managed.

A Bookstore on the Campus

Harald Bohne

It is evident that in order to carry out its full obligation as a publisher the University of Toronto Press must seek the widest possible distribution for its own scholarly publications; as operator of its own bookstore, however, it is also actively engaged in the selling of books from many other publishers. Toronto's dual rôle of wholesaler and retailer of books is unique among the fifty-odd member institutions in the Association of American University Presses. Nevertheless, publishing houses such as Doubleday and Scribner do operate their own retail outlets in addition to issuing formidable lists of their own publications, thus increasing the book outlets for all publishers.

How is it possible to account for the separation of university presses and university bookstores which is normal in North American university communities? The answer is that a university press is interested in selling books exclusively; college "book" stores in North America have too often degenerated into general department stores where practically any commodity except automobiles and real estate may be purchased. Many university stores have become big business with big profits, and because of the relatively marginal net income available from the selling of books, the book departments of these stores have often contracted into mere service departments for the sale of text-books to students. It would be highly inappropriate for a university press to extend its administrative activities to such an operation; at the same time, the manager of a college store would draw little advantage from association with a university press.

This is not to say, however, that the "general store" trend at many institutions has developed without criticism. Educators, students, publishers, and booksellers themselves have been loud in its condemnation. The 1961 Convention of the National

Association of College Stores stressed as its main theme the importance of "book-centred" college stores. Three of the major speeches delivered at this meeting were concerned with this same question: what are the functions of a university bookstore?

It is sometimes not appreciated that a campus bookstore has educational obligations towards the university community, and that these can be as important as those of an academic department. In a society in which books have lost their central significance, in which the reading and discussion of books no longer is entirely fashionable, the university must instil in its students a feeling for the importance of reading, and a delight in the pleasures to be found in good literature. The bookstore most certainly can play a rôle in this phase of university education. In some respects it can do this even more effectively than the library, because it not only stresses the importance of books, but the importance of owning books, of building a personal library, of cultivating a taste for collecting books. Students go through university at a time of their lives when their attitudes in such matters are still pliable; it is at university that they become fully accustomed to using books, and may come to love and respect them as well. If at this stage the campus store does not fulfil its obligations, it will miss an important opportunity to provide a permanent cultural service. If, however, a campus boasts a truly well-stocked bookstore, good reading habits may be formed, and many students be encouraged to adopt the custom of buying and reading books, and to continue it after graduation.

A college bookstore should also feel a strong attachment to the faculty and administrative staff of the university it serves. One of its functions should be to provide a showroom for new and old publications of significance in the various disciplines. It is to be admitted that a bookstore will never entirely discharge this responsibility, but it should not cease striving to do so. In the process, the staff of the university will come to recognize that the bookstore is more than a mere "students'" bookstore—it exists for their use as well. It is, of course, a cliché to note that books cannot be sold unless they are shown. But the bookstore on the campus can be the showplace for every important book, new and old, which should be of interest to any group in a university community. This must be its aim, even though space limitations and the abundance of new publications may make it difficult to realize the objective completely.

In order to discharge its purpose adequately, a college bookstore should not attempt merely to duplicate the function of commercial bookstores in the same community. Because of the specialized interests of its audience, it can sell many books that will never be carried by other booksellers. On the other hand it should not necessarily seek to have every book which one would expect to find in a commercial bookshop. One might, however, reasonably expect to find in a Canadian college bookstore a good stock of cultural and technical books, a select list of current and standard fiction titles, a rather good supply of Canadiana, and possibly, a small selection of children's books and de luxe editions.

It is clear that a university bookstore has a responsibility to act as much more than a text-book servicing centre—a function that could be discharged through a wicket, or possibly even automated by the use of requisition cards. True, the stocking and distribution of text-books is an important function, and one that a university bookstore must constantly be alert to provide to the very best of its ability. It may even be necessary for a well-stocked store to stream-line its operation at rush seasons to permit the most efficient possible distribution of text and reference books. The fact that a university bookstore conducts approximately one-third of its total annual business within a period of six weeks in the autumn illustrates the fact that seasonal peaks are one of the big problems in the organization and management of a college store. The store must therefore be laid out in a way that allows maximum flexibility. The movable display stands and showcases which occupy approximately 3,000 square feet in the centre of the University of Toronto Bookstore, have been designed to permit dismantling and storage in the basement within four hours by the regular sales staff. Such flexibility also allows frequent changes in the layout of the store during the year, be it to make room for special book exhibits or to give emphasis to a particular section at a particular season.

Another aspect of the operation of a university bookstore is its duty to offer a complete service for special book orders. Although the University of Toronto Book Department carries over 15,000 titles, it is impossible to stock all books that may be required at all times, and because of the demand for highly specialized books, the special book order department has become an important feature of the bookstore. The University of Toronto Book Department has placed as many as 1,700 special orders in one month with various publishers. These, it must be understood, are orders for single copies of specialized reference works which are not normally stocked by any bookstore. The importance—and the overhead cost—of this department is indicated by the fact that it employs three full-time researchers whose responsibility it is to check in publishers' catalogues and various reference books the information received from the customer, to keep in constant touch with publishers, and to report to customers regarding the numerous separate shipments involved.

Thus, a university bookstore may provide a wide variety of services, including those of a cultural and educational bookstore, a service centre for text-books and for students' supplies, and a clearing-house for special orders. From these functions stem many related activities. The University of Toronto Book Department, for instance, also acts as a purchasing agent for books ordered by various departmental libraries on the campus; it sells stationery and office supplies to university departments; it operates a periodicals subscription department for faculty members and departments; and, as an additional outgrowth of the special order department, it processes a great many book orders received by mail. These orders arrive from all over Canada and often originate from graduates of the University of Toronto who have remained customers of the bookstore.

The success of a university bookstore depends to a great extent on the quality of its communications with faculty and staff. It would be impossible for any bookstore to operate a text-book department without the full co-operation of the faculty, which recommends the text-books used by the student body. The preparation and evaluation of the resulting estimates of text-book requirements each summer is one of the important duties of a college store operation. Books must be ordered from the publishers many months in advance of college opening. Otherwise reports of books "temporarily out of print" will plague bookstore and faculty alike, even to the point that courses must be re-scheduled. Because of the variety of titles listed for required reading in some faculties, and because of the uncertainty of availability of used books (other than those purchased every spring by the bookstore itself), a university bookstore must take a considerable although calculated risk by stocking large quantities of a great many titles.

There are other ways in which a university bookstore can serve the university community and, possibly, the community at large as well. One area is that of the serious periodical; very few communities have a news-dealer indulgent enough to sell literary quarterlies, scholarly university journals, "little" magazines, foreign periodicals, and newspapers and journals of serious comment and criticism. Displays of foreign books, of standard works on a given subject, of books published by other university presses, of art books, of books on typography and typographic *tours de force*, are contributions the bookstore can make. Even small art exhibits, lectures, poetry and dramatic readings, and chamber music recitals, are activities the university bookstore might consider as part of its rôle as a cultural centre. As long as these endeavours play their part in the dissemination of knowledge by means of the written word, they have a place in the bookstore on the campus.

The advent of the quality paperback has opened an important new area of service for the campus store, and one which it is peculiarly well able to fill. The paperback indeed is tailor-made for the university bookstore: it is easy to handle, it does not occupy much room, it is pre-priced, serially numbered, and sold at regular trade terms; the selection of titles now available in paperback is directly aimed at the prospective student buyer, and includes the type of book one would expect a university student to buy. Most important, paperbacks are sold at prices that students can afford to pay. They possess the further advantage of making it possible for the campus store with little space and capital to provide a wide selection of distinguished authors, thereby helping the bookstore to play its full part in the education of the students on its campus.

There are, of course, some communities that are blessed with excellent commercial bookstores which can fulfil the rôle of the university bookstore. But in general, commercial and university bookstores have a place side by side, and have no good grounds for being jealous of each other. In effect, they are both working towards the same higher objective; the student who has bought his first books in his college bookstore will eventually become a good customer of other bookstores. The very existence of a bookstore presupposes a literate public, and the cultivation of literary appreciation is perhaps the greatest service that a college store renders. Consider, for example, a community of a quarter of a million inhabitants. Among these might be numbered between 15,000 and 20,000 regular book-buyers. Such a select group is actually being served and encouraged in its reading habits by the University of Toronto Book Department.

Ainsworth, R.
Aitken, I.
Albin, H.
Albrant, Mrs. I.
Allen, K.
Allen, R.
Arthur, Mrs. M.
Atkinson, Mrs. F.

Baker, T.
Balogh, Mrs. E.
Beaven, E.
Bell, W.
Bishop, K.
Bland, J. C.
Bohne, H.
Booth, G.
Booth, H.
Bott, Miss P.
Brockett, Mrs. M.
Brown, Mrs. B.
Brown, G. W.
Budd, W.

Campbell, J.
Carey, Mrs. E.
Chambers, Miss E.
Chetcuti, S.
Clark, Miss D.
Clark, Miss E.
Clark, Miss E. L.
Cochrane, Miss H.
Cook, Mrs. E.
Cooper, A.
Cooper, Mrs. J.
Cosgrave, B.
Cowling, T.

D'Agnone, A.
Davidse, J.

Davidson, R. I. K.
Dewan, Miss J.
Doyle, D.

Ecclestone, A.
Ecclestone, J.
Eng, H.
Enright, Mrs. C.
Erickson, D.
Eva, W.

Fearnside, E.
Fee, L.
Field, A.
Findlay, J.
Fisher, Miss M.
Flatt, Miss W.
Fraser, W.

Garden, J. G.
Godfrey, R.
Grabowski, G.
Grant, Mrs. B.
Grant, L.
Grant, Mrs. N.
Grice, Mrs. J.
Gurney, R.

Halasz de Beky, Mrs. A.
Halpenny, Miss F.
Hamelin, M.
Hamm, D.
Hanna, D.
Hansen, J.
Harman, Miss E.
Hartmann, Mrs. G.
Hawkins, B.
Hawkins, Mrs. N.
Haynes, H.
Henderson, Mrs. A.

Hendry, H.
Hendry, Mrs. R.
Hern, J.
Hill, Mrs. A.
Hoff, Mrs. I.
Holmes, Mrs. M.
Horne, E.
Hornyansky, Mrs. W.
Houston, Miss J.
Hubbard, Mrs. E.
Humphrey, W.
Hutchison, Miss E.

Ivanoff, Mrs. I.

Jamieson, Miss J.
Jeanneret, M.
Johnson, Mrs. D.
Jones, Mrs. E.

Keiser, Mrs. G.
Keller, Mrs. E.
Kenneth, C.
Kewageshig, W.
Knechtel, J.
Koenig, F.
Kruberg, Miss G.
Kurschenska, H.

LaPierre, Mrs. P.
Law, Mrs. E.
Linge, W.
Lingner, Miss A.
Little, P.
Loosley, Miss E.
Louden, Mrs. E.
Lubowski, G.
Luciani, L.

Mackenzie, Mrs. A.
MacMurray, Miss M.
Magee, Mrs. M.
Mahl, Mrs. M.
Malcher, F.

Mallon, J.
Marescaux, Mrs. S.
Marosi, V.
Marshall, H.
Martin, Mrs. L.
McCarthy, Miss J.
McCartney, B.
McConnell, Mrs. L.
McCormack, W.
McCuaig, F.
McDonough, J.
McFarland, Mrs. C.
McIvor, Miss R.
Metz, F.
Midtun, Miss B.
Miller, J.
Miville, Mrs. H.
Mohs, C.
Monet, J.
Moore, E.

Neal, R.
Nelson, J.
Newel, D.
Newman, E.
Norris, Mrs. J.
Northover, Mrs. C.

O'Mahony, P.
Ottaway, E.
Ourom, Miss L.

Pagnello, Mrs. E.
Pedersen, S. A.
Perry, Mrs. M.
Peters, A.
Pidgeon, R.
Plewman, Miss B.
Pryde, Miss D.

Redhill, S.
Reid, D.
Reid, Miss M.
Reilly, Miss P.

Revell, J.
Rhodes, Miss J.
Rigby, Mrs. A.
Risebrough, Miss E.
Robinson, L.
Ross, W.
Rowles, W.
Rushton, J.

Sayliss, Mrs. E.
Saywell, Mrs. P.
Saywell, W.
Schutte, Mrs. U.
Sheldon, Mrs. K.
Sherman, W.
Shred, A.
Siegel, J.
Sigurjonsson, Miss A. K.
Skeats, S.
Skrabik, T.
Small, G.
Smith, R.
Sommer, Mrs. M.
Stephenson, Mrs. D.
Stevenson, Mrs. G.
Stewart, Miss J.
Strutt, F.
Sutton, Mrs. B.
Swanston, Mrs. M.

Tanner, W. A.
Taylor, J.
Taylor, R.

Thomson, J.
Tiley, Miss B.
Toth, L.
Towne, Mrs. E.
Trimble, N.
Tyler, C.

Vassilev, Mrs. J.
Verrall, A.
Verrall, Miss G.
Vierlinger, Miss D.
von der Marwitz, Mrs. E.

Waisberg, Mrs. S.
Walker, F.
Warkentin, Mrs. G.
Warner, Mrs. L.
Watson, Mrs. L.
Wells, Mrs. C.
Weston, F.
White, N.
Wild, E.
Williams, K.
Wilson, C.
Wilson, Miss E.
Wilson, J.
Wilson, Mrs. M.
Woodland, R.
Woollon, L.
Wyatt, C.

Zahra, F.
Zemell, Miss B.

This book has been set in Monotype Bembo with Bembo display type.

Design: Harold Kurschenska, MTDC

Lightning Source UK Ltd.
Milton Keynes UK
UKHW010000210722
406167UK00001B/254

9 781487 591366